OPPORTUNITIES IN

ELECTRONIC DATA PROCESSING

by Martin Nussbaum

Vocational Guidance Manuals

EDUCATIONAL BOOKS DIVISION OF
UNIVERSAL PUBLISHING AND DISTRIBUTING CORPORATION
NEW YORK

Library of Congress
Catalog Card Number 73-184503

VOCATIONAL GUIDANCE MANUALS
Published by Universal Publishing and
Distributing Corporation
235 East 45 Street
New York, N.Y. 10017

Manufactured in the
United States of America

ABOUT THE AUTHOR

MARTIN NUSSBAUM is president of Computamation, consultants in the edp (electronic data processing) field in the areas of publishing, advertising, public relations, and marketing.

Previously, he was editor for five years of *Data Processing Magazine,* which he helped build into a major national trade publication. His concern for the industry, and his well-received monthly editorial, "On Line," led one letter writer to label him "the conscience of the industry." The name has stuck ever since. He is able to draw on the friendship of many important people in the edp field.

After graduation from Temple University in 1952 with a B.A. in communications, Nussbaum was involved in the reform movement in Philadelphia, spending a short time in local politics and city government. He began a newspaper career as a reporter/rewriteman on weeklies (becoming editor of one) and moving up to copy editor and rewriteman for the Philadelphia *Daily News.*

Subsequently, the author entered the technical writing field, where his strong scientific/technical background and writing ability combined to earn a high reputation for him. He helped write some of the early aerospace documentation on Atlas, Tiros,

Discoverer, and other projects and has worked on technical documentation in the computer field. He has held positions with General Electric, RCA, Philco, and Univac.

Mr. Nussbaum has taught Fundamentals of Technical Writing, Creative Writing, Design and Layout, Navigation, Electronics, Communications, and other subjects, and has lectured on various aspects of edp to trade groups, professional societies, etc.

A senior member of the Society of Technical Writers and Publishers, the author was chairman of the Delaware Valley Chapter for two years. He is also a member of the Institute of Electrical and Electronic Engineers, and was chairman of the Philadelphia Chapter, IEEE Group on Engineering Writing and Speech, for three years.

Mr. Nussbaum is also a member of the Association for Computing Machinery, the Data Processing Management Association, the American Society for Cybernetics, the American Society for Information Science, the IEEE Computer Society, the American Institute of Aeronautics and Astronautics, and the American Business Press.

PREFACE

MAN IS INCLINED to define the time in which he lives by naming it after the objects or forces which have the greatest effect on him. It is safe to say, therefore, that we are living in the age of the computer. For no other technical development or human concept has brought such rapid change and is having such profound and far-reaching effects on our everyday lives.

In little more than 20 years, the computer has pervaded almost the entire fabric of our life. There is very little we do today that is not influenced or controlled in some manner by a computer. Today, computers run trains, operate telephone switching networks, set newspaper type and control printing, operate traffic light systems, control light and power generators, prepare payrolls, check inventories, provide engineering information for automobile and aircraft design, assist physicians in diagnoses and lawyers in preparing briefs, provide high-speed information retrieval from libraries, help football coaches scout their opposition, monitor space flights and lunar landing sites, register automobiles and birth certificates, and are involved in hundreds of other applications. And there is every indication that our interface with and dependence on the computer will increase in the coming years. One can predict with certainty that there will be some type of computer in almost every home.

With this burgeoning use of the computer has come an attendant need for people. As new applications for it are being developed each year, thousands of job opportunities are being created to design, build, sell, and operate newly-required computers. Thus, there has always been, and will continue to be, a need for trained personnel; and one of the industry's consistent problems has been finding and training the people to fill these available jobs.

Honeywell's vice president Robert P. Henderson does not overstate the need when he says "the data processing industry's most pressing challenge is to find and train the thousands of men and women who will be needed to fill the openings in the next decade."

Robert E. McDonald, executive vice president of Sperry Rand, and former president of Sperry Rand's Univac Division, is also concerned about the need for people, optimistically so. "If you are looking for an exciting, meaningful career, the data processing industry has the elements which can spell success," he says, adding ". . . [it] is not only the fastest growing area of our technological society, it is a field with worldwide impact. You can become deeply involved in a technology which is helping . . . change our worldwide way of life in many . . ways." Above all, he feels, "[edp] is a field with a future," for "one of the most attractive facets of [edp] is the wide range of opportunities available. . . ."

Because the computer industry has grown so rapidly in so short a time (it has expanded an average of 20 percent in each of the past five years), there is a shortage of accurate statistical data on equipment and manpower. However, most authorities agree there are approximately 65,000 to 75,000 computers of all types installed in the U.S. today. These include everything from the desk-top minicomputer on up to the gigantic CDC

7600 installed in the Lawrence Radiation Laboratories in Livermore, California. The worth of these machines range between $25 to $30 billion. Compare this with the dozen or so computers installed in 1950.

The future holds even more promise. Estimates of the number of computers to be installed by 1975 range between a conservative 120,000 to an optimistic 200,000.

But employment tells the story better. There are approximately 700,000 people working directly with computers (operators, programers, analysts, designers, marketing people, etc.) today. Another 500,000 will be needed by 1975. And, of course, this number does not include the thousands of retail clerks, stock brokers, educators, scientists, manufacturers, researchers, etc., who will need to operate computers.

There is no doubt that skilled data processing personnel will be in great demand in the coming years. Nor is there any doubt that, because of its diversity and glamor, data processing will continue to offer challenge and satisfaction.

M.N.

CONTENTS

INTRODUCTION

Advances in technology have always been accompanied by a changing world and changing patterns of employment. The industrial revolution saw the launching of a mass migration from the farming communities into the newly developing industrial centers and the beginnings of an ever-increasing class of blue-collar workers. The advent of the automobile provided an answer to the growing concentration of cities; inexpensive individual mass transportation led first to the unfolding of urban suburbia and then to the modern sprawling ubiquitous exurbia.

The advent of the computer has caused a similar revolution in the ranks of the white-collar worker. Major changes have taken place in the handling of information; the proportion of clerical help in business offices has shrunk either by attrition through not hiring replacements or simply by letting people go. In their place has grown a large population of computer specialists who design, program, operate, and maintain the thousands of computer systems in industry and government throughout the United States and the rest of the world. The application of computers continues to grow in our modern technological society and the demand for personnel continues to grow in proportion in order to keep our computers running.

The magic of computers ("Do computers really think?") and the mystery of their operation have led to a large collection of books describing the hardware and software characteristics of these modern machines. But the aptitudes and skills of the people needed to program and operate them have received significantly less attention. This important book by Martin Nussbaum is unique in that it concentrates on the human side of the electronic data processing world.

Opportunities in Electronic Data Processing is a comprehensive compendium of factual information to help the young man or woman who is seeking a place in the electronic data processing field. Here in one place is a description of the kinds of work and the kinds of people who have made successes for themselves by programing, operating, and managing computer systems. The duties, educational requirements, aptitudes, and temperaments required for each job category have been spelled out with the detail and care that is typical of the author's previous works.

Martin Nussbaum learned a great deal about electronic data processing as editor of *Data Processing Magazine,* where he was exposed to the day-to-day problems of the computer world. His emphasis in this book on education and training and on the schools, societies, organizations, and information sources for the computer field are a reflection of his growing greater concern for the human element in the computer field.

The discussion of electronic data processing and the way computers work is deliberately brief, but it is nevertheless effective. The detailed listing of junior colleges, colleges, universities, and correspondence schools is a particularly valuable aid. Written by an expert with many years of direct involvement as a spokesman for the field, this book is sure to be an invaluable aid also to everyone involved in the management, operation, and use of computers and electronic data processing systems.

MORRIS RUBINOFF, Ph.D.
Professor, Moore School of Electrical Engineering,
    University of Pennsylvania
President, Pennsylvania Research Associates

(Dr. Rubinoff designed the first Philco computer.)

CHAPTER 1

ELECTRONIC DATA PROCESSING — A NEW CAREER

ELECTRONIC DATA PROCESSING is one of the few professions or industries that was in large measure created and shaped by its chief tool—the computer. Any understanding must then begin with this most important implement, the object which structures the industry.

The terms *computer* and *electronic data processing* (edp) are often used synonymously, but there is a difference. Data processing is the procedure of collecting, rearranging, processing, and presenting of data for further use. Data is defined as a representation of facts, concepts, or instructions; expressed directly or as numbers, letters, or symbols that can be communicated and interpreted so as to form conclusions.

Early data processing was accomplished on mechanical devices such as calculators and accounting machines, or on electromechanical devices known as tabulating equipment. These operations were known as automatic data processing (adp). With the advent of modern electronic computers, the adjective "automatic" was changed to "electronic." Because a computer ingests, processes, and either stores or spews out large quantities of data electronically, a computer performs electronic data

13

processing. By extension, one can speak of the computer industry or the edp industry.

WHAT IS A COMPUTER?

A COMPUTER is a combination of many rather basic components. Like a modern skyscraper, it looks imposing as a unit. Yet the skyscraper consists of nothing more than simple building blocks—perhaps a dozen—used repetitively in the thousands. The computer, in like manner, consists of components connected to form larger assemblies. It is important to view a computer in this manner so that you will understand that it is only an electromechanical contrivance. It cannot think or act independently in any manner more creatively than any of man's other machines and implements. It depends upon man to initiate its actions and to guide it through its work patterns. If a computer seems to act ingeniously, it is only because man is making it do so. If a computer performs a certain task formerly performed by a man, it is only because the computer's designer built it that way. If a computer performs a dull, routine, physically taxing job formerly performed by a man, it is to man's benefit. Certainly the automobile, or the typewriter, or the sewing machine have not replaced man. A computer cannot replace a creative, *thinking* man. On the contrary, with the increase in automation has come an ever-increasing demand for people to design the computers, write their programs, sell and service them, and interpret their data.

HOW A COMPUTER DOES THE JOB

THE DIGITAL COMPUTER is designed to recognize only two states or conditions of any proposition, action, quality, measurement, etc. These states can be *on* or *off, true* or *false, yes* or *no, presence of a signal* or *absence of a signal, 1* or *0, 7 inches* or *not 7 inches,* and so on. But this principle can be used to do a wide variety of jobs.

Let's see how, with an example. Assume that the United States Navy is building a new submarine rescue ship—one that can descend to the ocean floor and rescue men trapped within a submerged and damaged submarine. The Navy needs qualified and experienced men to command and operate the craft, so the Bureau of Naval Personnel is put to work to find these men. A list of qualifications is prepared which includes experience and prior duty in submarines, rescue and salvage operations, and communications. Some of the crew should have paramedical training, and frogman or skin-diving training. Knowledge of hard-hat diving equipment is also an asset. There are certain physical and medical requirements. Altogether, some 20 specifications are established, and the search begins. The Bureau of Naval Personnel must now literally sort through the tens of thousands of personnel records it has on file on every person within the Navy to see who will fill the bill. This is a laborious and time-consuming job by hand, a simple job by computer.

Assume further, for this illustration, that the Navy has a punched card for each member on active duty. The card contains information on education and prior training, a medical history, personal characteristics, and other important facts. A computer is programed to accept a card if it finds a hole in that card to indicate prior submarine experience. If no hole appears (indicating no prior submarine experience), the card is rejected. At the same time, another section of the computer is looking for a hole to indicate paramedical training. In all, 20 sections of the computer are looking for holes. We can program the computer to put all cards with 20 holes in one pile and the balance of the cards in another pile. Or, all cards with 20 holes in one pile, all cards with 19 holes in a second pile, all cards with 18 holes in a third pile, and so on. Either job will be completed in a short time with all the information arranged in convenient categories. And a great deal of work has been saved, or rather performed, by the computer. Though this has been a simple example, the same basic principles illustrated here are used no matter how complex the computer operation may get.

THE INDUSTRY

THE EDP FIELD is concerned with the acquisition, processing, storage, and retrieval of information; the control of industrial and other processes; mathematical, scientific, and engineering computation; and system design. It makes use of computer systems; keyboards, visual displays, and other peripheral equipment; supply items, such as cards, paper tape, magnetic tape, and disks; repository equipment, such as microfilm/microfiche devices; test equipment; software (the programs or instructions which operate the computer); systems-related accessory equipment, such as filing systems; and numerous services, such as design engineering, system analysis, programing, consulting, education, and marketing.

The edp field is known as a *horizontal* industry to indicate that the use of data processing is not confined to one segment of our society. *Vertical* industries, on the other hand, are characterized by rather specific training, orientation, working conditions, social outlook, and so on. An example of a vertical industry would be pharmacy, where one's training is fairly well standardized, one's work is generally performed in a retail drug store or ethical drug manufacturer's facility, and one's duties are more or less patterned.

In edp, however, there are no bounds. A geologist could use a computer to search for oil; a personnel manager could use a computer to locate a job prospect; a diplomat can have translations produced by computer. Scientists at the Smithsonian Institution can identify incoming specimens with a computer; teachers can utilize edp for instruction, test scoring, and classroom assignment. Sculptors and musicians use computers to create fine arts. Computers are used by weathermen, stock brokers, insurance men, legislators, and grocery clerks. Truly, the computer is a universal tool.

HISTORICAL BACKGROUND

THE MODERN ELECTRONIC COMPUTER was born in 1946 at the University of Pennsylvania's Moore School of Electrical Engineering. The brain child of John W. Mauchly and J. Presper Eckert, ENIAC (for Electronic Numerical Integrator And Computer) was designed or use by the U.S. Army Ordnance Department to compute firing tables for artillery weapons. It began operating in August 1947 at the Army's Aberdeen Proving Ground. Construction took 2½ years, requiring the soldering of a half-million connections from 18,000 vacuum tubes. ENIAC consumed 200,000 watts of power and weighed 30 tons. But what a worker. In a second it could perform 5,000 additions. In 10 seconds it could compute a shell trajectory—a task that formerly took 20 hours on a desk calculator. And in two hours it could solve complex equations in atomic physics—a full year's work for 100 engineers. However, ENIAC had one drawback, if one could use that term. All of its programs had to be hand-wired by plug boards and external switching.

It remained for the next computer, EDVAC (*E*lectronic *D*iscrete *V*ariable *A*utomatic *C*omputer), to change that. Designed on principles advanced by John von Neumann, and on which most present computers are based, EDVAC was the first electronic computer to have its program wired or stored internally. Its completion in 1952, also by Eckert and Mauchly, marks the beginning of the programing profession. For with EDVAC one no longer had to be an electronics engineer to be able to program. The requirements changed to logical reasoning ability and an understanding of problem solving.

Computers are divided by their design into generations. Other important first- and second-generation computers were SEAC at the National Bureau of Standards (1950), Whirlwind I at MIT, UNIVAC (*UNIV*ersal *A*utomatic *C*omputer) designed by Eckert and Mauchly (1951), the Institute of Advanced Study Computer designed by von Neumann, the IBM 701 brought out in 1953, and the 650—the first mass-produced modern computer. The early 1950s marked the entry into the field of such large manufacturing firms as IBM and Remington-Rand. IBM introduced two of the most famous second-generation systems in 1959—the 1401 and the 1620. IBM is also generally credited with bringing out the first third-generation machine—the System 360, which appeared in 1964. It ushered in the use of microelectronic circuits to replace transistors, and thereby reduced the physical size and power consumption of computers.

THE FUTURE

THERE HAS BEEN SOME INDICATION in the past two years that a fourth generation in computer design is upon us. However, many believe its introduction will not be sudden,

A typical large computer center, featuring a Univac 1108 system which can process data from several users simultaneously. While computer operator sits at console, sorting machine operator (left) processes punch cards, peripheral equipment operator (rear) mounts one of 5,000 customer programs, and computer operations supervisor (right) tends magnetic tape drive. Programer (center) discusses data with customer over phone.

but evolutionary—occurring over a period of several years. The fourth generation will be marked by miniaturization and new design concepts rather than new theoretical approaches—the primary reason being that there is too much money invested in present equipment to make it obsolete this quickly.

Rapid strides in large-scale integration—a method for miniaturizing many large components on tiny circuit boards—should augment a trend away from large central computer systems toward desk-top minicomputers or satellite terminals and graphic display units. More and more, computers will be connected to telephone lines and provide almost instantaneous interchange of large quantities of data. This concept in data communications may change many of our present life patterns radically. For example, we will use the telephone to borrow library books, select merchandise at retail stores, obtain newspapers, have physical examinations, receive computer-assisted instruction, request stock market quotations, and transact computerized banking.

There is every indication that the gap is narrowing between symbolic or machine language used by the computer and our everyday spoken language. This development will permit many more people to have hands-on experience with computers, and accelerate the trend toward a computer in every home.

GENERAL RETURNS TO BE EXPECTED

A CAREER IN EDP will offer many returns to those willing to apply themselves and persevere toward their goals. First, there is the satisfaction of working in a glamorous and exciting field, in the forefront of technology, enjoying a high status. New advances are made constantly, bringing new challenges with them.

Second, the opportunities for advancement are unexcelled. There are no closed doors. Today's programers are tomorrow's systems analysts and edp managers. In a field where the need for people increases each year, the only limiting factor is one's own ability. When a firm's profit and loss is dependent upon an edp operation, there is no place for prejudice of any kind. Sex, skin color, or religion are unnoticed. Too, knowledge of edp permits easy entry into other fields. Many financial vice presidents, directors of engineering, or marketing managers will make their marks first in edp. For dynamic change means fewer entrenched people.

Third, the pay scale is generally higher in edp than in other fields. This will continue to be the case as long as there is a shortage of trained, competent people.

Fourth, edp offers above average security. As the number of installations increase, and as your experience and skills improve, there will always be a need for you.

NECESSARY PERSONAL ATTRIBUTES

SO DIVERSIFIED IS THE FIELD that there are jobs in edp for almost everyone, provided he or she has or obtains the proper education and training. There are no restrictions. Sightless and other handicapped people, for example, have made and are making excellent programers. Each of us can bring his own talents and experience to the field, thereby enriching it. However, there are general characteristics of personality, education, and training that make one more suited to certain broad categories of positions.

If you have a logical mind, can analyze problems, can attend to details, and are good with figures, you would do well to investigate the general area of software design and programing. A facility for symbolic logic and languages may augur well for you specifically in computer langauge development.

If you are machine-oriented, electromechanically inclined, or enjoy equipment design, you might find yourself drawn to hardware design.

An outgoing personality and the desire to work with people might suggest management or marketing. While an interest in concepts or ideas might lead you into applications or planning— the use of computers to solve the problems of our cities, environment, politics, education, etc.

Whatever your background and interest, edp can use you. In the following chapters we will examine in more detail the types of jobs encountered in edp, the education and training necessary to qualify you for them, and how to go about obtaining them. We hope this information will help you to decide about your career in edp.

CHAPTER 2

THE PEOPLE INVOLVED

THE EDP INDUSTRY has had a double effect on employment. Not only has it created many entirely new occupations, it has also brought about new and additional duties for many existing occupations. Such jobs as systems analyst or sorting-machine operator were unheard of before the advent of the computer, while others, such as computer design engineer or computer salesman, are highly specialized and unique occupations adapted from previously established ones.

Whenever a computer is built, more jobs are created. For the computer is only a tool; it is dependent upon people to design it, build it, apply it, maintain it, program it, and utilize it. Thus, a relationship between the computer and man exists in some manner in almost every job in edp. For convenience, we can group these job relationships in six broad categories.

COMPUTER SYSTEM PRODUCERS

THIS GROUP CONSISTS OF those who research, design, and build computer systems, and develop related edp products and services. Generally, people in this group work in a manufacturing facility, or are faculty members of universities who conduct research in their schools' laboratories.

Some of these people are involved in basic research in electronics, physics, or related sciences. Others may evolve systems of computer mathematics and languages. Some may devote their time to applied research to create better materials and processes. Finally, there are those who combine all this preliminary work into the design and manufacture of specific computer systems and products, and into the development of computer languages and software (the instructions and programs which operate the computer).

Many of the occupations in this group predate the computer, but have evolved because of the computer into newer, more unique jobs. Because there is less standardization of duties in this group, occupation titles tend to be less formalized.

The researchers, developers, and designers include scientists, mathematicians, applied mathematicians, research and development engineers, computational linguists, programers, systems analysts, and college and university professors and instructors.

The builders include design engineers, production engineers, electronic technicians, plus all those generally found in a manufacturing facility—operating and test engineers, quality control engineers, etc.

COMPUTER SYSTEM MARKETERS

ALMOST ALL THE PEOPLE in this group work directly for manufacturers. There are systems and application engineers who search for new uses for computers, and marketing researchers who show where markets exist for new systems. There are advertising and public relations personnel who promote the company's name and products. Also, and extremely important, there are the actual computer salesmen. They are usually well trained in both computer applications and marketing. Usually, too, they're specialists. Each will concentrate in scientific or business applications, or he may limit himself to a specific industry.

As in the first group, most occupations here tend to have predated the computer. However, they have undergone vast changes. A computer salesman, for example, is a more sophisticated, knowledgeable, scientifically oriented breed than his counterpart in other fields. He may have a college degree in business or engineering or both.

COMPUTER SYSTEM INSTALLERS AND MAINTAINERS

WITHIN THIS GROUP are those people who actually install computers and teach the users how to operate them. Also included are those who keep the computers operating and service them. Here, too, most of the people are employed by the manufacturers.

As we get closer to the user, we find that occupations tend to be newer, and duties tend to be more uniform or standardized. Some occupations in this group still predate the computer, but others were unheard of until recently.

Agreement on titles for these relatively new occupations usually does not occur immediately. Consequently, we may have several titles describing the same job. For example, Burroughs and Univac call their maintenance men *field engineers*. Honeywell refers to them as *service engineers*. To IBM they are *customer engineers*; to NCR they are *technical service repre-sentatives*; while at RCA they are known as *computer service representatives*.

SUPPLIERS OF SUPPORT PRODUCTS AND SERVICES

SUPPORT PRODUCTS include auxiliary equipment (also referred to as peripheral equipment) which is attached to com-puters such as tape transports and terminals, or items used in the computer installation such as punch cards, paper and mag-netic tape, and forms. Support services are provided by software developers and consulting houses. Purchase of these products and services generally occurs after the computer is installed, though many times consultants will help select the computer.

Occupations within this group are similar to those in the preceding three groups except the overall work operation is on a smaller scale. We have people designing, developing, and building support equipment. There are marketers, installers, and maintenance people. Perhaps only in the area of services is there some difference. Companies developing programs, or offering consultation and similar services, usually are organized to spe-cialize only in that one area, as opposed to being attached to and supporting a large manufacturing company. But occupations in a service company are identical to others in the industry. We will see systems analysts, programers, machine operators, and so on.

EDUCATORS

THOSE WHO TEACH PROGRAMING, computer sci-ences, or other allied courses in public and private schools, universities, or in industry, belong in this group. They are characterized by a deep interest in edp, usually a working experience in the industry, and they devote the greatest portion of their working time to the teaching of edp subjects.

COMPUTER SYSTEM USERS

THIS GROUP CONTAINS by far the largest number of people. Their work is performed in one of the many computer installations throughout the country, ranging from the small one- or two-man operations up to those employing hundreds of people. The installation could be part of a large industrial company, a commercial airline, a retail store, a university, a governmental agency, a service bureau, a time-sharing facility, and so on. It is safe to say that the occupations within this group were created as a direct result of the computer. Occupational duties and titles are just about standardized from installation to installation.

Occupational titles within this group include applications engineer, business programer, chief business programer, card-tape converter operator, coding clerk, computer electronics mechanic, computer operations supervisor, computer operator, data typist, detail programer, edp manager, engineering analyst, engineering and scientific programer, high-speed printer operator, keypunch operator, operations research analyst, peripheral equipment operator, project director, sorting-machine operator, systems analyst, systems engineer, tape librarian, and verifier operator.

PATTERNS EVOLVED

AS WE SAW, THE COMPUTER either transformed older occupations or created newer ones. Also, an occupation may have several similar, but different titles, depending upon the preference of the employer. Finally, duties of many occupations can be performed in more than one environment. A programer, for example, can work for a manufacturer, as a computer system producer; for a software developer, as a supplier of support services; or for a retail department store, as a user.

We will discuss the newly created occupations in detail, and list their alternate titles, in the following chapter. The balance of this chapter will be devoted to a short description of the life cycle of a computer system, from development to usage, so that we can better see how the occupations in the six categories will interact with the computer in many ways.

DEVELOPING THE COMPUTER SYSTEM

THE IDEA FOR A new computer system begins in many cases with the marketers. Salesmen returning from the field report a need going unfilled. They sense that they could probably sell a computer system if it had certain capabilities. If there appears to be enough demand, the sales manager will confer with the marketing director, who in turn will begin holding meetings with applications engineers, software developers, research engineers, and top management. An attempt is made to alter or adapt an existing computer system to do this new job. Sometimes all that is needed is new software. However, if a present system cannot be modified, or if modification will not produce the desired results, a new computer may be called for.

Many times, the impetus for a new computer will come from the research staff, who will develop a new process or component, or unearth a new scientific principle. Such "breakthroughs" almost always result in new computer systems, because they produce more product for less money. Before the "go ahead" is given to build a new system, a marketing study is made to see if there are enough potential purchasers in the market place to justify the new development. In some cases, only *one* potential customer is needed to set the gears in motion. For example, the Atomic Energy Commission in Livermore, California, may need a huge specialized computer system costing millions of dollars. The contract to build this one-of-a-kind computer may be bid on by several manufacturers.

Once the market is established and the decision to proceed is made, the engineering department begins designing and constructing a prototype (the first engineering model). Engineering holds many close conferences with the program development group, frequently designing to meet software goals. The research department may be involved with developing some new material for the computer's memory, or a new process to plate a magnetic disk. Others—scientists, mathematicians, language experts—are also consulted.

When the prototype is finally built, checked out, and accepted, the manufacturing department begins to work. Production procedures are established, component parts are ordered or built, and technicians and other workers are hired to assemble the new computer systems. Meanwhile, new programs to operate the system are being written and checked out by many different levels of programers. Technical writers are writing assembly procedures, checkout procedures, operators' instruction manuals, troubleshooting procedures, and so forth.

Before the first computer comes off the assembly line, the marketers are busy. The public relations group sets up press conferences and industry previews to announce the new computer, and prepares brochures, booklets, and other printed material explaining all the technical details needed by industry writers to prepare articles and columns. The advertising department is planning its campaign in the communications media. The actual marketing people are renting exhibit space at conventions and conferences to show the computer and answer questions about it for prospective buyers. The salesmen themselves are learning about the new system, and are even trying to get some advance orders. Also, the training department is preparing curricula and training programs to teach future programers and operators how to use the newly designed equipment.

After a period, computers begin coming off the assembly line and, hopefully, orders for them are being sent in by the salesmen. Selling a computer is an involved and lengthy job. Depending upon the size of the system, a salesman may work with a prospective customer for months or even years before the sale is made. He may work with a systems engineer or alone in developing a special installation or designing new work procedures for the user. The systems engineer may spend most of his time before the sale, for many months after the sale, or equally in both periods working with the customer. He is employed by the manufacturer to solve a customer's problem in information handling and control. He spends a great deal of time in the customer's facility, asking questions, observing operations—in fact, almost learning the company's business. When he has thoroughly analyzed the situation, he develops procedures and recommends equipment to do the job.

Installing a computer involves more than plugging it in. Again, depending on size, as many as a dozen or more people may be involved. Sometimes months of continual effort are devoted. In addition to the actual hookup and complex wiring, there are many checkout procedures, preliminary tests, and start-up procedures to run. The installation team may include the systems engineer, one or more customer or field engineers, and one or more instructors. The customer or field engineer, in addition to actually installing the equipment, has the responsibility for maintaining the equipment at maximum efficiency. For as many years as the equipment is operating, he will perform routine inspections, answer the customer's calls for service, install modifications, and do any other jobs required to keep the computer system functioning.

If the new computer system is small, the customer may send his system analysts, programers, and operators to the manufacturer's schools to be trained to use the equipment, or to increase their skills generally. If the new computer system is large, it may be more convenient and economical for the manufacturer to send one or more instructors to the customer's installation.

STAFFING THE COMPUTER CENTER

WITH THE COMPUTER INSTALLED and ready to function, qualified people will be needed to perform the many duties necessary to operate the system efficiently and profitably. To help us visualize these duties better, let us pretend we are staffing a large data processing center containing several general purpose computer systems. Our organization chart will look like this:

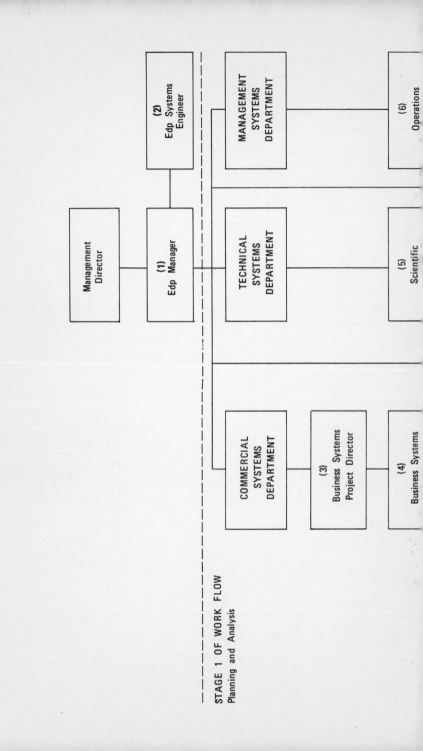

STAGE 1 OF WORK FLOW
Planning and Analysis

Programing

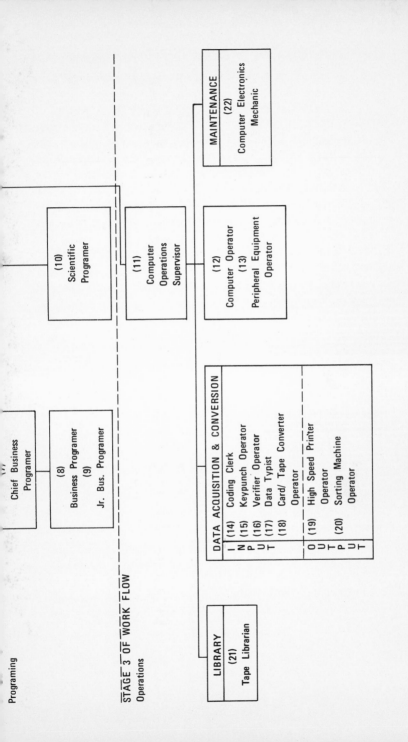

Chief Business Programer

(8) Business Programer
(9) Jr. Bus. Programer

(10) Scientific Programer

STAGE 3 OF WORK FLOW
Operations

(11) Computer Operations Supervisor

(12) Computer Operator
(13) Peripheral Equipment Operator

MAINTENANCE
(22) Computer Electronics Mechanic

DATA ACQUISITION & CONVERSION

INPUT
(14) Coding Clerk
(15) Keypunch Operator
(16) Verifier Operator
(17) Data Typist
(18) Card/ Tape Converter Operator

OUTPUT
(19) High Speed Printer Operator
(20) Sorting Machine Operator

LIBRARY
(21) Tape Librarian

The chart is divided horizontally into three sections to illustrate the three stages of work flow involved in the processing of data through the computer center. Numbers are used to indicate 22 basic occupations defined by the United States Department of Labor. They will be described in more detail in the following chapter.

The *edp manager* (1) has charge of the entire computer center and usually reports directly to management. It is his job to see that work flows smoothly from one department to another and is finshed within a reasonable time. He confers with the *edp systems engineer* (2) on system requirements, placement of new equipment, and other similar matters. The edp systems engineer, as we saw earlier, usually works for a manufacturer or consulting firm. He is included here because his work environment is the computer center, and his is one of the newly created occupations.

The edp manager evaluates all work entering the computer center to be processed; determines whether the data is a) commercial, b) technical, or c) management in nature; then assigns it to the proper department or individual. He must make this initial determination for a very sound reason. Though a general purpose computer is designed to handle all three types of applications, systems analysts and programers are trained to specialize in only one area. Background, education, and training requirements are different for each type of work. Jobs which are concerned with computing payrolls, keeping inventory records, billing, analyzing sales, and addressing mailing labels are referred to as commercial or business applications. Jobs which are concerned with solving mathematical equations, determining chemical processes, solving problems in physics, and determining missile trajectories and satellite orbits are referred to as technical or scientific applications. Jobs which are concerned with man-

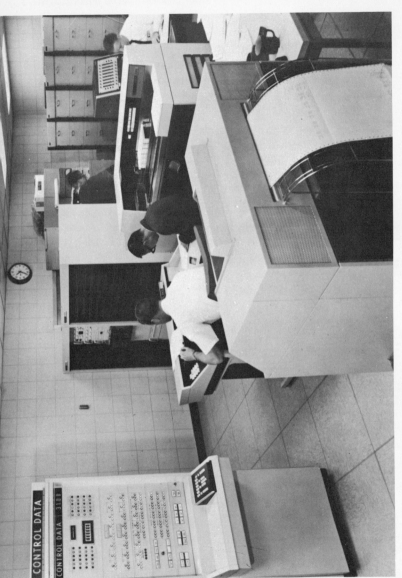

The Control Data 3100 is a typical medium-size scientific computer system. A scientific programer consults with a scientific systems analyst in the center foreground, as a tape librarian (rear) catalogs programs, and a coding clerk (right) records codes on a worksheet.

agement problems, such as marketing analyses, work scheduling, and profit and loss, are referred to as management or operations research applications. Business applications, by far the most numerous of the three types, are characterized by large quantities of input and output data involving comparatively little internal processing. Consequently, business applications give rise to clearer demarcation of duties, and call for larger work areas with more peripheral devices. Scientific applications are characterized by small quantities of input and output data, but involve a great deal of internal processing. Scientific applications thus give rise to overlapping of duties, less differentiation between occupations, and require smaller work areas. Operations research applications, though gradually gaining in importance, are still relatively small in number. They are really a form of commercial data which provide information to management helpful in making decisions. Usually only one or two people are assigned to operations research.

PLANNING AND ANALYSIS

AFTER EVALUATION by the edp manager, the data to be processed enters stage 1 of the work flow. This stage, known as problem planning and analysis, is concerned with analyzing the data and the problem, determining the cost of machine time and man-hours required, and establishing the methods and procedures to do the job. Business applications are routed to the Commercial Systems Department, scientific applications to the Technical Systems Department, and management applications to the Management Systems Department.

Because the Commercial Systems Department is several times larger than the other two departments combined, it has an additional level of supervision. The *business systems project director* (3) plans, directs, and reviews all the projects within the department. He coordinates the activities of *business systems analysts* (4), and may schedule and assign duties to the *operations research analyst* (6). Usually, though, the operations research analyst and the *scientific systems analyst* (5) work with a minimum of supervision, reporting directly to the edp manager. Regardless of the department in which they work, systems analysts collect facts concerning the information needs of the computer user, and analyze these facts. They then formulate efficient procedures of data flow from originating sources to the computer, chart the computer operations necessary to convert the raw data into meaningful information, and finally plan the distribution and use of the information evolved.

PROGRAMING

STAGE 2 OF THE WORK FLOW—programing—involves taking the work of the systems analyst and preparing it for use on the computer. It falls to the programer to convert the analyst's solution for a problem into a detailed plan for solution by the computer. This detailed plan is a series of logical steps or computer instructions called a "program," which makes the computer perform the desired operations. Computer instructions received by the programer are in natural or spoken language. However, a computer is designed to act in "machine language" which is a set of procedures expressed in the number system basic to the computer, together with symbolic operation codes. "Programing languages" are designed to bridge this gap. Some programing languages such as COBOL (which stands for *CO*mmon *B*usiness *O*riented *L*anguage), are almost similar to natural English. The programer must be aware of the many languages available and be proficient in several. Designing the program for a large project may take many months to a year, and the program may be several volumes thick. It consists of flow charts (graphic representations of the processing sequence), and the procedural steps themselves, both of which show how the data will flow through the computer and what actions are to be performed at each step along the way.

Business programing, like business systems analysis, has several levels of responsibility. The *chief business programer* (7) plans, schedules, and directs the operation of the business programing section. He supervises and reviews the work of the *business programer* (8) and the *junior business programer* (9). The *scientific programer* (10) usually works with a minimum of supervision.

OPERATIONS

THE OPERATIONS PHASE—stage 3 of the work flow— is concerned with the actual machine operations involved in processing the data and obtaining the solution. The program or computer instructions and the data to be processed are now prepared for entry into the computer by the *coding clerk* (14), the *keypunch operator* (15), the *verifier operator* (16), the *data typist* (17), and the *card/tape converter operator* (18). The coding clerk prepares the data for the keypunch operator and the data typist. He uses a coding system distinctive to the computer in use to convert routine information from records and reports into machine-language codes. The keypunch operator takes this coded information, and using a machine similar to an electric typewriter, transfers the coded information to punch cards by punching the appropriate holes. These are the same punch cards we used to solve our Naval Personnel problem in Chapter 1. The verifier operator uses a similar keypunching machine to verify the accuracy of the data punched on the punch cards. The data typist takes the coding clerk's coded information and transfers it onto paper tape, magnetic tape, or punch cards using any one of a number of terminal devices or perforating devices. The duties of a keypunch operator and a data typist are similar, and in many computer centers the titles are used interchangeably to describe the same occupation. However, to be precise, the keypunch operator usually specializes in operating the keypunch machine. The card/tape converter operator operates a machine that automatically transcribes data from punch cards to reels of tape, or from tape to punch cards. Depending upon the type of problem presented to the computer, the program, and other factors, either punch cards or tape may be used as input to the computer. In many cases both are used.

When the program and input data are in the proper form, they are loaded on to the computer's input units by the *computer operator* (12), who then initiates the processing and monitors the operation. In large installations the computer operator is assisted by a *peripheral equipment operator* (13) who will load magnetic tape units, place punch cards in hoppers, position magnetic disks, place optically coded or magnetically coded cards on card readers, and so on.

Upon completion of the processing cycle, the computer presents the solution (known as the *output*) to the problem in one or more ways. By display on a television tube; by recording on magnetic tape; by printing on a high-speed printer; by sorting punch cards into several groups; by tracing drawings on a plotter; etc. In large installations the printing operation is handled by the *high-speed printer operator* (19), while the punch card sorting operation is handled by the *sorting machine operator* (20). The program is not discarded, as it can be used again for similar problems. It is sent to the library where the *tape librarian* (21) catalogs and stores it for future use.

As you can visualize, all the operations in stage 3 must be coordinated efficiently if the work flow is to function smoothly. Computer time is very expensive; if the computer is not working because it lacks some input or because it needs servicing, operating costs will skyrocket. The individual responsible for seeing that things run smoothly, is the *computer operations supervisor* (11). In addition to scheduling the flow of work and the usage of the machines, he keeps production records, prepares budget estimates, supervises the various workers, and recommends needed equipment.

In small computer centers, the actual repair and maintenance is performed by the manufacturer's customer or field engineer. In large installations, this work is performed by a *computer electronics mechanic* (22), who is part of the operations staff.

Now that you've had an overall view of computer development and usage, and learned, perhaps to your amazement, of the amount and variety of jobs in edp, you're probably wondering which one is for you. The next chapter will help you decide. We'll explore in more depth those newly-created occupations shown on our organization chart on pages 32-33. We will not discuss those previously existing occupations such as teaching, selling, or engineering, which have been modified into newer edp careers. Entire books have been devoted to these older, basic professions. We will follow the lead of the U.S. Department of Labor, which devotes its 72-page brochure, *Occupations in Electronic Computing Systems* (listed in the bibliography in Appendix A), to coverage of the new occupations only, considering them "to be the basic occupations most directly concerned with electronic computing." A knowledge of these basic occupations will help you understand what edp is all about. It will then be relatively easy to augment this comprehension with information pertinent to your specific interests.

CHAPTER 3

DESCRIPTION OF JOB CLASSIFICATIONS

THE OCCUPATIONS LISTED HERE are considered to be the basic occupations most directly concerned with edp. In a field that is still young and changing, titles, duties, hiring requirements, and other qualifications are not yet standardized. Consequently, there is a degree of overlap and duplication in duties and responsibilities. Titles, too, are not consistent throughout the industry. We have used those titles which are the most commonly accepted, following them with alternate titles by which they are also known. The occupations are arranged according to supervisory responsibility and work flow as indicated on the organization chart in Chapter 2. Information on wages has been compiled from several sources and extrapolated by the author. These sources include the U.S. Department of Labor's *Occupational Outlook Handbook* and *Monthly Labor Review,* the annual EDP Salaries Report sponsored by the monthly industry trade journal *Business Automation,* the *Survey of Information Processing Personnel* conducted by several professional societies and sponsored by the Advanced Research Projects Agency of the Department of Defense, reports of the Bureau of Labor Statistics of the U.S. Department of Labor, and others. The salary ranges listed indicate the *average* low to the *average*

41

high reported; they do *not* indicate the lowest or highest salaries reported. Also, bear in mind that the lower end of the range indicates the salary paid to a novice, while the higher end of the range reflects several years of experience in the occupation.

EDP MANAGER

Alternate Title: Data Processing Director

Duties: Directs and coordinates the activities of the edp division. Consults with management to determine priorities of various projects, to discuss purchase of new equipment, and to determine requirements of other divisions. Establishes work standards; assigns, schedules, and reviews work; interprets policies, and goals of organization to subordinates; and prepares progress reports for management. Reviews reports of equipment production, breakdowns, and maintenance. Interviews and hires subordinates, directs their training, and determines their promotion.

Education, Training, and Experience: Graduation from high school, plus two years of formal education in edp, or equivalent practical experience, is necessary for small computer installations. Courses should be in business administration and accounting, or engineering. A college degree in one or more of the above fields is preferred for large installations. Experience in systems analysis, programing, and computer operations is desirable. In installations offering higher level services, such as operations research and engineering applications, a college mathematics major coupled with experience listed above is desirable.

Aptitudes: Verbal ability to translate technical terminology into terms understandable to management and department heads.

Numerical ability to understand mathematical problems and applications.

Spatial ability to read engineering drawings, charts, and diagrams.

Interests: An interest in scientific and technical subjects to cope with the wide range of technical and scientific problems processed through the computer. An interest in business or management to understand departmental operation and the marketing of services.

Temperaments: Ability to deal effectively with people, to understand problems of superiors and subordinates, to make judgments or decisions calmly under pressure, and to influence superiors and motivate subordinates.

Physical Activities and Working Conditions: Work is sedentary and performed inside. Much time spent in conferences either explaining or evaluating ideas. Occasional walking to various departments and offices.

Salary: Average ranges between $1,230 to $1,870 per month.

EDP SYSTEMS ENGINEER

*Alternate Titles: Computer Systems Engineer,
Edp Methods Analyst*

Duties: Analyzes edp projects to determine equipment requirements, continually updates his knowledge of availability and characteristics of new equipment on market, and plans layout of computers and peripheral equipment to achieve efficient operation and effective use of assigned space.

Education, Training, and Experience: A college degree in electronic engineering is usually required. Additional training in business administration or industrial management is desirable to understand problems of computer users. Approximately one year of formal training by a computer manufacturer is the usual method of entry into this occupation. Experience in systems analysis, programing, and operations could be an alternate requirement.

Aptitudes: Verbal ability to write reports of findings and recommendations, to discuss problems with management and department heads in language understandable to them, and to read manufacturers' manuals and related technical magazines and publications.

Numerical ability to understand mathematical and technical problems of systems analysis, programing, and operations.

Spatial ability to visualize layout of equipment.

Interests: An interest in scientific and technical subjects to understand computer systems and their application. A preference for business contacts with people to exchange information with management and users.

Temperaments: Requires ability to deal tactfully with people such as managers and supervisors to discuss problems and obtain information.

Physical Activities and Working Conditions: Work is sedentary and performed inside. Some walking and standing is required when surveying accommodations for equipment layout.

Salary: Average ranges between $1,120 to $1,680 per month.

BUSINESS SYSTEMS PROJECT DIRECTOR

Alternate Titles: Business Data Processing Project Director, Business Systems Coordinator, Lead Analyst, Program Manager, Project Planner, Senior Business Systems Analyst

Duties: Plans, directs, and reviews business applications projects assigned to business systems analysts. Prepares progress reports. Trains junior analysts, and assists others in various phases of problem analysis, solution outlining, solution detailing, program coding, and "debugging" (eliminating errors).

Education, Training, and Experience: A bachelor's or master's degree in business administration, with courses in accounting, mathematics, or statistics often is required. Employers frequently waive academic training requirements for currently employed workers possessing extensive experience in systems analysis, design, and supervisory responsibility. Employers frequently require a degree or equivalent experience either in industrial engineering, or the engineering field most directly related to their manufacturing processes, if their edp system is used for production forecasting, planning, and control.

Aptitudes: Verbal ability to obtain information, and discuss project plans, problems, and progress.

Numerical ability to analyze problems and develop statements capable of being programed.

Spatial ability to develop or interpret work flow diagrams and charts.

Interests: A preference for activities that involve contact with others. An interest in business management and the use of computer systems to solve its problems.

Temperaments: Ability to perform a variety of duties involving frequent change. Must be able to assign subordinates on the basis of their specializations and abilities, and control activities through personal contact and reports. Required to make decisions of judgment.

Physical Activities and Working Conditions: Work is sedentary and performed inside. Some walking and standing is required to coordinate work activities of others.

Salary: Average ranges between $1,150 to $1,680 per month.

BUSINESS SYSTEMS ANALYST

*Alternate Titles: Commercial Systems Analyst and Designer,
Data Methods Analyst, Systems and Procedures Analyst*

Duties: Collects and analyzes facts concerning business problems. Formulates efficient patterns of information flow from source to computer. Defines the computer process necessary to change raw data into useful information. Plans the distribution and use of resulting information. Develops process flow charts or diagrams, first in outlined form, then in detailed form for programing and for checking. May work as member of team or alone. In smaller computer installations the functions of the systems analyst and programer are frequently combined, while in the larger installations the functions are separate.

Education, Training, and Experience: A college degree with courses in business administration and accounting is usually required for those without prior experience in edp. Some employers, while requiring a degree, do not require a specific major or course content. Many employers waive the formal education requirements for those business programers who through experience have acquired a background in business systems and procedures. Currently, the trend is to require a knowledge of advanced mathematics. Continuing education, through specialized courses, self-study, and participation in professional associations, is the rule rather than the exception.

Aptitudes: Verbal ability to discuss problems and progress, and to prepare reports.

Numerical ability to analyze problems and develop statements capable of being programed.

Spatial ability to visualize and prepare graphic representations of work flow.

Form perception to identify symbols.

Interests: A preference for activities or games that are analytical, abstract, or creative in nature.

Temperaments: Ability to confer with, and interview others. Ability to reason logically and to make decisions of judgment when confronted with several alternatives.

Physical Activities and Working Conditions: Work is sedentary and performed inside. Occasional handling of documents, charts, and other records.

Salary: Average ranges between $800 to $1,100 per month for a junior systems analyst, and between $950 to $1,490 per month for a systems analyst.

SCIENTIFIC SYSTEMS ANALYST

Alternate Titles: Applied Mathematician, Computational Engineer, Computing Analyst, Engineering Analyst I, Engineering-Scientific Systems Analyst

Duties: Formulates mathematical models of scientific, engineering, and other technical problems for solution by computer. Analyzes problems such as "figure out the best design for a ballistic missile." Consults with technical personnel to prepare mathematical equations. Searches library for appropriate mathematical formulas and other data pertinent to the problem. Converts analysis to computer form using such languages as FORTRAN (which stands for *FOR*mula *TRAN*slator).

Education, Training, and Experience: A college degree with emphasis on mathematics and the physical sciences is the minimum requirement. Graduate training, and practical experience in one of the fields of engineering or physics, is especially

The Burroughs B 5700 is a medium-scale computer system with many peripherals. In the foreground, a peripheral equipment operator is running a batch of cards through the card reader. On the right, a computer electronics mechanic is monitoring a routine test program at the control panel. In the rear (left), a programer checks data with a systems analyst.

desirable. It is necessary to continue education on a part-time basis to be informed of continuing changes and new techniques. Some knowledge of technical programing techniques is essential.

Aptitudes: Verbal ability to interpret technical data and discuss problems with project originators.

Numerical ability to analyze problems and prepare mathematical formulas to handle them.

Spatial ability to understand blueprints, drawings, and diagrams.

Form perception to detect differences or similarities in groups of symbols, performance curves, and similar data.

Interests: A preference for activities that are technical or mathematical in nature.

Temperaments: Ability to engage in a variety of activities during the course of one assignment. Such activities would include problem analysis, engineering consultation, library research, review of computer output, etc.

Physical Activities and Working Conditions: Work is sedentary and is performed mainly, but not completely, inside.

Salary: Average ranges between $1,000 to $1,570 per month.

OPERATIONS RESEARCH ANALYST

Alternate Titles: Management-Operations Analyst,
Operations Analyst

Duties: Formulates mathematical models of management problems in order to solve them on a computer. Provides solutions for planning, forecasting, and making decisions. Gathers or researches data. Specifies the methods or formulas to be used in the processing operation. Prepares written, nontechnical reports to management indicating specific solutions or a number of possible alternatives.

Education, Training, and Experience: College degree with emphasis on advanced mathematics and statistics is usually the minimum requirement. A combination of advanced degrees in mathematics and business administration is especially desirable. A doctorate in mathematics is frequently required. Specific training in operations research at graduate school is becoming a standard requirement, as more universities offer courses in this area. Many workers have acquired the necessary background in mathematics through education and experience in engineering and the physical sciences, and knowledge of special techniques through self-study.

Aptitudes: Verbal ability to understand the technical languages of various professional fields such as engineering and accounting, so as to prepare nontechnical reports for management.

Numerical ability in specialized areas of mathematics such as statistics and probability theory.

Spatial ability to prepare and interpret charts, diagrams, and graphs.

Interests: A preference for activities that are analytical or mathematical in nature, especially as they apply to management.

Temperaments: Ability to perform a variety of tasks on any particular assignment, either alone, or as a member of a team. Ability to converse with personnel on all levels and in several fields.

Physical Activities and Working Conditions: Work is sedentary and performed inside. Some walking between departments is necessary.

Salary: Average ranges bewteen $1,050 to $1,650 per month.

CHIEF BUSINESS PROGRAMER

*Alternate Titles: Computer Programing Coordinator,
Lead Programer, Programing Manager*

Duties: Plans, schedules, and directs the preparation of programs to process business data. Consults with managerial and systems analysis personnel to determine program intent, problem areas, and coding techniques. Assigns, coordinates, and reviews work of programing personnel. Develops own programs and routines. Consolidates segments of program into complete sequence of terms and symbols. Breaks down program and input data for successive computer passes. Analyzes test runs on computer. Revises or directs revision of existing programs. Compiles documentation of program development. Trains subordinates in programing and program coding. Prepares records and reports.

Education, Training, and Experience: Usual requirement is graduation from a technical school or college with training in business administration, computer programing, data processing mathematics, logic, and statistics. Usually, a minimum of two years' experience in programing on a particular computer is required. Experience in complex projects is an asset, as is knowledge of work flow, and a record of proven ability to supervise others.

Aptitudes: Verbal ability to present oral and written reports, and to read technical literature about changes in techniques and equipment.

Numerical ability to program in linear and Boolean algebra (the mathematics of logic).

Spatial ability to interpret general and detailed computer flow charts and diagrams.

Form perception to see details in charts and code sheets composed of symbols.

Interests: A preference for activities that are technical, that require problem solving, and that require logical thinking.

Temperaments: Ability to maintain good relations with superiors and subordinates. Ability to maintain direction of several projects being worked on simultaneously. Ability to impart training to subordinates.

Physical Activities and Working Conditions: Work is sedentary and performed inside. Some walking and conference attendance is necessary.

Salary: Average ranges between $1,060 to $1,500 per month.

BUSINESS PROGRAMER

Alternate Title: Digital Computer Programer

Duties: Converts symbolic statements of business problems to detailed logical flow charts for coding into computer language. Analyzes all or part of work flow chart or diagram to see how it can be adapted to computer's capabilities. Uses symbolic logic to develop sequence of program steps. Writes detailed, logical flow chart in symbolic form to represent work order of data to be processed by the computer system, and to describe input, output, arithmetic, and logical operations involved. Devises sample input data to test program, and observes or operates computer to run test. Prepares written instructions (called a "run book") to guide operating personnel during production runs. May specialize in writing programs for one make and type of computer.

Education, Training, and Experience: High school graduation mandatory, plus six months to two years of technical training in computer operations and in general principles of programing and coding. Current trend is to hire college graduates with training in accounting, business administration, and mathematics; provide them with a year of on-the-job training to qualify them for programing; then move them on to higher-level positions. In installations concerned with applications in market research or statistical forecasting, a college degree in mathematics is preferred.

Aptitudes: Verbal ability to understand oral or written statements concerning a variety of business problems, and to discuss them with others.

Numerical ability to interpret work flow charts and to understand machine logic.

Spatial ability to visualize or interpret diagrams.

Form perception to see detail in symbols.

Interests: A preference for activities that are technical in nature, or that require logical reasoning.

Temperaments: Ability to make rational decisions, to translate complex ideas into basic patterns, and to work patiently to solve problems.

Physical Activities and Working Conditions: Work is sedentary and performed inside. Moderate amount of communicating with others such as coding clerks and operating personnel.

Salary: Average ranges between $770 to $1,240 per month.

JUNIOR BUSINESS PROGRAMER

Alternate Titles: Detail Programer, Program Coder

Duties: Selects symbols from coding system of particular computer in use, and applies them to successive steps of completed program for conversion to instructions understood by the computer. Records symbols on worksheet for transfer to punch cards or tape. Confers with senior programers or computer operators to clarify portions of program. Usually works as understudy to the business programer.

Education, Training, and Experience: Must be high school graduate. Some training in programing, coding, and computer operations is preferred, but six months of job experience in company operations, work flow, standards, and terminology is the minimum requirement. One to four weeks of classroom training in coding for a specific computer is usually provided by employer or computer manufacturer. Some employers favor college graduates in order to enhance the worker's promotion potential.

Aptitudes: Verbal ability to recognize programing and coding languages consisting of abbreviated words, groupings of numbers, and symbols.

Numerical ability to convert decimal numbers to other number systems.

Form perception to recognize and remember graphic symbols.

Interests: A preference for activities of a routine, concrete, and organized manner.

Temperaments: Ability to perform repetitive tasks according to set procedures. Required to work to precise and established standards of accuracy.

Physical Activities and Working Conditions: Work is sedentary and performed inside.

Salary: Average ranges between $640 to $920 per month.

SCIENTIFIC PROGRAMER

Alternate Titles: Engineering Programer, Technical Programer

Duties: Converts scientific and other technical problems to format capable of processing by computer. Prepares logical flow charts and diagrams. Uses advanced mathematics to code equations for solving. Confers with engineering and other technical personnel to resolve problems. Observes or operates computer during testing or computer runs to analyze and correct programing and coding errors. May specialize in one type of application.

Education, Training, and Experience: Minimum requirement is usually a college degree with a major in mathematics or engineering. A master's degree or doctorate in mathematics or engineering is a common requirement where work is extremely complex or involves basic research in mathematics or programing. From two to four years of on-the-job training is regarded as necessary to become familiar with at least one class of computer, programing language, and application area. One- to four-week training sessions are given by employers and computer manufacturers to provide basic training or (later) specialized training.

Aptitudes: Verbal ability to discuss problems and equipment requirements, to prepare written records and reports, and to comprehend technical publications.

Numerical ability to interpret formulas, select equations, and use codes.

Spatial ability to prepare flow charts, diagrams, and other graphic data.

Form perception to see pertinent detail in diagrams, charts, and drawings.

Interests: A preference or activities technical in nature.

Temperaments: Ability to make judgments based on fact, or on past decisions. Ability to reason logically, and think through a complex situation to its basic operation.

Physical Activities and Working Conditions: Work is sedentary and performed inside. Conferring and collaborating with other technical personnel.

Salary: Average ranges between $890 to $1,510 per month.

COMPUTER OPERATIONS SUPERVISOR

Alternate Titles: Chief Console Operator, Senior Console Operator, Data Processing Supervisor, Edp Supervisor

Duties: Supervises and coordinates the activities of workers who operate edp equipment. Assigns personnel and schedules work flow. Directs training or trains personnel in operation of computers and peripheral equipment. Works with programers in testing new and revised programs. Aids operators in locating and overcoming error conditions. Prepares or reviews records and reports of production and operation.

Education, Training, and Experience: High school graduation is the minimum requirement. Usually one to three years' experience in operating computers and peripheral equipment is required. Additional prerequisites are familiarization with programing and coding techniques; these can be gained through experience in computer operation or a course in programing. However, a two-year post-high school training course in edp may reduce experience requirements. Training in business administration, mathematics, and accounting is regarded as particularly desirable. Some employers require a college degree, particularly in large installations where duties are mainly administrative or supervisory.

Aptitudes: Verbal ability to train and supervise subordinates, and prepare records and oral or written reports.

Numerical ability to comprehend program being run.

Spatial perception to prepare wiring diagrams, wire control panels for peripheral machines, and operate equipment.

Interests: A preference for activities that are technical in nature.

Temperaments: Ability to perform a variety of tasks subject to frequent change. Ability to plan and direct the activities of others, and to deal with people such as other departmental supervisors. Ability to make decisions of judgment.

Physical Activities and Working Conditions: Work is light, requiring frequent standing and walking, and is performed inside. There is occasional lifting and handling of reels of tape, decks of punch cards, and control panels.

Salary: Average ranges between $900 to $1,290 per month.

COMPUTER OPERATOR

Alternate Titles: Console Operator, Digital Computer Operator

Duties: Monitors and controls computers according to operating instructions. Sets control and operating switches on computer and peripheral equipment. Selects and loads input and output units with materials such as tapes, punch cards, printout forms, etc. Observes machines and control panels for error lights and printout messages. Clears equipment at end of operating run and reviews schedule to determine next assignment. Records operating and down-time (that period when the computer is not running or operating).

Education, Training, and Experience: A high school education is the minimum requirement, but an increasing number of employers are demanding an additional several months to two years of technical school training in edp. This training usually includes such courses as computer mathematics, accounting, business practices, elementary programing, and operation of computers and peripheral equipment. The employer or computer manufacturer usually provides one to three weeks of formal

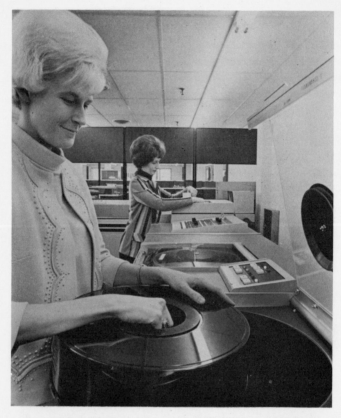

In smaller facilities, such as this NCR Century 100 installation, duties frequently overlap. While the programer
(front) changes one of the magnetic disk memory units,
the computer operator places punch cards in reader.

instruction for the specific computer system the worker will operate. On-the-job training ranges from a few months to one year.

Aptitudes: Verbal ability to comprehend technical language of operating instructions and equipment manuals.

Numerical ability to prepare operating records, to time computer runs, and to comprehend operating processes.

Spatial perception to wire control panels for peripheral equipment.

Form perception to identify flaws in input and output materials.

Motor coordination to set up machines, to move keys and switches, and to respond to error conditions.

Interests: A preference for working with machines and in technical activities.

Temperaments: Ability to perform a variety of tasks, sometimes at the same time, subject to frequent change. Ability to follow written and oral instructions.

Physical Activities and Working Conditions: Work is light, and performed inside. Requires frequent standing and walking when loading and monitoring equipment. There is frequent lifting and handling of reels of tape, decks of punch cards, and control panels.

Salary: Average ranges between $485 to $920 per month.

PERIPHERAL EQUIPMENT OPERATOR

Alternate Titles: Assistant Console Operator, Tape Handler

Duties: Operates auxiliary equipment to transfer data from one form to another, to print output, and to read data into and out of computer. Mounts and positions materials, such as reels of magnetic or paper tape onto spindles, decks of punch cards in hoppers, bank checks in reader-sorters, or output forms in printing devices. Sets guides, keys, and switches according to instructions. Observes materials for creases, tears, or printing defects; and watches machines and error lights to detect machine breakdowns. Unloads and labels card or tape input and output and places them in storage or routes them to library. Separates and sorts printed output forms.

Education, Training, and Experience: High school graduation is minimum requirement. Post-high school training in operation of electronic or edp equipment is desirable. Employers frequently regard worker as understudy to computer operator and apply the same education requirements to him.

Aptitudes: Verbal ability to read written instructions and handbooks.

Spatial ability to follow diagrams to wire control panels, position and thread tapes onto spindles, or position decks of punch cards in hoppers.

Motor coordination and finger and manual dexterity to load and unload machines quickly, to thread ribbons of tape over guides and through rollers, and to handle cards and tapes deftly.

Interests: A preference for working with machines and in technical activities.

Temperaments: Must be adept at performing a variety of tasks requiring frequent change to operate a number of machines in varying combinations and sequences.

Physical Activities and Working Conditions: Work is light, involving frequent standing and walking, and is performed inside.

Salary: Average ranges between $465 to $720 per month.

CODING CLERK

Alternate Titles: Junior Programer, Programer Trainee

Duties: Converts routine items of information from records and reports into codes for processing by the data typist or keypunch operator. Manually records alphabetic, numeric, or alphanumeric (containing both alphabetic and numeric) codes in prescribed sequence on worksheet or margin of source document for transfer to punch cards or machine input tape. May be designated according to trade name of computer system as Coding Clerk, Univac; or IBM Coder.

Education, Training, and Experience: High school graduation is mandatory. Training of a day or two in a classroom or under the direction of an experienced worker usually is provided by the employer. Achievement of adequate speed, and particularly the development of a high degree of accuracy, takes from one to three months. Achievement of speed involves the memorization of many of the codes.

Aptitudes: Verbal ability to understand written and oral instructions, business terms, and abbreviations.

Interests: A preference for activities of a routine, concrete, organized nature.

Temperaments: Ability to tolerate repetitive work activities or of a short cycle in nature.

Physical Activities and Working Conditions: Work is sedentary and performed inside.

Salary: Average ranges between $465 to $665 per month.

KEYPUNCH OPERATOR

Alternate Titles: Cardpunch Operator, Printing-Punch Operator

Duties: Operates keypunch machine to transcribe data from source material onto punch cards, and to reproduce prepunched data. Attaches skip bar to machine and previously punched program card around machine drum to control duplication and spacing. Loads machine with decks of punch cards. Moves switches and depresses keys to select automatic or manual duplication and spacing. Inserts previously punched card into card gauge to verify registration of punches. Observes machine to detect faulty feeding, positioning, ejecting, or skipping.

Education, Training, and Experience: High school graduate preferred with proficiency in typing. High school or business school training in keypunch operation is desirable. Frequently, one week of training is provided by employer or manufacturer of equipment.

Aptitudes: Verbal ability to understand oral and written instructions, such as manufacturers' operating manuals.

Motor coordination to read work sheets and simultaneously operate keyboard of approximately 40 keys. Finger dexterity to move switches on machine.

Interests: Preference for organized and routine activities.

Temperaments: Ability to perform repetitive duties. Ability to follow specific instructions and set procedures.

Physical Activities and Working Conditions: Work is sedentary, with infrequent lifting of decks of cards to load machine, and is performed inside.

Salary: Average ranges between $380 to $570 per month for junior to intermediate level keypunch operators, and between $460 to $750 per month for senior to supervisory level keypunch operators.

VERIFIER OPERATOR

Duties: Verifies accuracy of data punched on punch cards, using keyboard-type machine that rejects incorrectly punched cards. Removes incorrectly punched cards as indicated by light or by key that will not depress. May punch corrected card using keypunch machine.

Education, Training, and Experience: High school graduate with proficiency in typing. High school or business school training in keypunch operations is desirable.

Aptitudes: Verbal ability to understand oral and written instructions.

Motor coordination to read work sheets and simultaneously operate keyboard of verifier.

Interests: Preference for organized, routine activities.

Temperaments: Ability to perform repetitive tasks, and to work to precise and established standards of accuracy.

Physical Activities and Working Conditions: Work is sedentary, with infrequent lifting of decks of punch cards, and is performed inside.

Salary: Average ranges between $375 to $520 per month.

DATA TYPIST

Duties: Converts alphabetic, numeric, and symbolic data into coded form on cards or tapes, using special-purpose electric keyboard machine. Loads decks of cards or reels of magnetic or paper tape into machine. Moves switches to set up machine and auxiliary equipment to produce desired cards or tapes. Proofreads typed copy to identify errors, and retypes copy or activates correctional devices built into machine. May insert tape or cards into reader attachment for automatic duplication of business correpondence or records. May be designated according to trade name of machine used, such as Unitypist.

Education, Training, and Experience: High school graduate with proficiency in typing. One week of on-the-job training usually is provided by employer or manufacturer of equipment to learn operation of machine. Up to three months of on-the-job training is usually given to become familiar with material typed, such as narrative and tabular forms, and programing languages.

Aptitudes: Verbal ability to recognize meanings of words, and to use and spell standard abbreviations.

Motor coordination to operate keyboard and load machine.

Interests: Preference for routine and organized activity.

Temperaments: Ability to perform repetitive typing duties. Must be able to follow oral and written instructions.

Physical Activities and Working Conditions: Work is sedentary and performed inside.

Salary: Average ranges between $410 to $620 per month.

CARD/TAPE CONVERTER OPERATOR

Duties: Operates machine that automatically transcribes data from punch cards to reels of tape, or from tape to punch cards. Wires plug board (similar to switchboard) to make connections according to prepared diagrams and to prepare data in desired format. Mounts reels of tape on spindles, places stacks of punch cards in hopper, and starts reading and recording machines. Observes operation of machines to detect malfunctioning. Marks identification on reels of tape or drawers of punched cards at end of run, and keeps control sheet.

Education, Training, and Experience: High school graduation or equivalent preferred. Experience is desirable in handling punch cards and in operating electromechanical machines such as sorters.

Aptitudes: Clerical perception to verify sequence of punch cards, and to record information on control sheet.

Motor coordination to wire plug boards and set up machines.

Interests: A preference for activities of a routine nature.

Temperaments: Adaptable to activities that are repetitive

and of a short cycle. Can work to established standards of accuracy.

Physical Activities and Working Conditions: Light work, performed inside. Stands and walks most of work period. Reaching, handling, and fingering is involved.

Salary: Average ranges between $390 to $560 per month.

HIGH-SPEED PRINTER OPERATOR

Alternate Title: Off-Line-Printer Operator

Duties: Operates high-speed printing machine to record output of computer or information previously recorded on reels of tape. Wires plug board to make connections according to prepared diagrams and to prepare data in desired format. Mounts tape reels on spindles and positions paper rolls on which data is to be printed. Observes printing for legibility, and panel lights for indications of errors. Removes printed sheets from machine and stores reels of tape.

Education, Training, and Experience: High school graduation, plus experience in operating machines such as keypuncher, verifier, and sorter.

Aptitudes: Verbal ability to understand written instructions and handbooks.

Clerical perception to detect errors in printing and format.

Motor coordination to wire plug boards and operate machine.

Interests: A preference for working with machines, and for activities that are routine in nature.

Temperaments: Ability to perform tasks which are repetitive and of short cycle. Ability to adhere to established standards of accuracy.

Physical Activities and Working Conditions: Work is light, and performed inside. Stands most of time. Lifts and carries drawers of punched cards and reels of tape.

Salary: Average ranges between $390 to $560 per month.

SORTING MACHINE OPERATOR
Alternate Title: Card-Sorting-Machine Operator

Duties: Tends machine that automatically sorts perforated punch cards into specific groups. Loosens cards to prevent over-feeding, and jamming, and places cards in feedbox. Pushes buttons on sorting control panel to regulate sorting process. Starts machine and sights through holes to verify sorting. Removes sorted cards from bins. Removes jammed cards to clear machine.

Education, Training, and Experience: High school graduation required. Usually, three months on-the-job training is necessary to learn machine operation and gain proficiency.

Aptitudes: Motor coordination to push buttons on sorting-machine control panel.

Manual dexterity to shuffle and handle cards.

Interests: Preference for activities of a routine, organized nature.

Temperaments: Ability to perform repetitive tasks of placing and removing cards, pushing control buttons, and starting machine. Ability to work under specified instructions with little independent action involved.

Physical Activities and Working Conditions: Light work, performed inside. Mostly standing, or moving about.

Salary: Average ranges between $390 to $560 per month.

TAPE LIBRARIAN

Duties: Classifies, catalogs, and maintains library of reels of magnetic or punched paper tape, or decks of magnetic or punch cards. Classifies and catalogs material according to content, purpose of program, routine or subroutine, and date on which generated. Assigns code conforming with standardized system. Prepares index card for file reference. Issues materials and maintains charge-out records. Inspects returned tapes or cards for signs of wear or damage.

Education, Training, and Experience: High school graduate, preferably with commercial background. Three to six months' experience as catalog clerk, file clerk, or mail clerk is desirable.

Aptitudes: Verbal ability to read information on labels describing contents of decks of cards and reels of tape, and ability to read catalogs that contain standard codes and abbreviations.

Numerical ability to perform inventory functions.

Interests: A preference for working with things and objects.

Temperaments: Ability to follow routine and organized patterns, and to follow established procedures.

Physical Activities and Working Conditions: Work is light, involving frequent standing and walking. Work is performed in library, but tape librarian may work in computer room performing such tasks as loading and removing printout forms, reels of tape, and decks of cards from machines.

Salary: Average ranges between $475 to $670 per month.

COMPUTER ELECTRONICS MECHANIC

Alternate Titles: Computer Electronics Specialist, Computer Serviceman

Duties: Repairs electronic computers and peripheral equipment following diagrams, schematics, and handbook instructions. Inserts test programs and data in computer, monitoring operation to determine cause of machine error or stoppage. Operates or observes computer and peripheral equipment during system tests to locate defective circuits. Uses test instruments to diagnose faults. Solders faulty connections and adjusts, repairs, or replaces defective components. Performs routine maintenance such as cleaning, replacement of worn parts, and lubricating of moving parts. Keeps maintenance records and maintains an inventory of replaceable parts.

Education, Training, and Experience: High school graduation, plus two years of technical school training in electronics is the usual requirement. Two years of college training in electrical engineering can be substituted for technical school training. Courses in computer theory, and repair of complex electronic equipment such as radar, is especially desirable. Manufacturers of computers and peripheral equipment often provide classroom and on-the-job training of up to one year in machine service and repair. This training usually includes operating, and at least rudimentary programing of the computer.

Aptitudes: Verbal ability to confer with operating personnel about processing errors and machine stoppage, and to understand technical handbooks and manuals.

Numerical ability to comprehend functions of computer.

Spatial ability to interpret displays on test equipment.

Manual dexterity to use hand tools.

Interests: A preference for activities of a scientific or technical nature, and a desire to build and repair electronic devices.

Temperaments: Ability to perform a variety of tasks, for working with hand tools and electronic equipment, and to make decisions concerning performance of equipment. Ability to reason logically and to diagnose so as to locate troubles. Ability to work to precise and established standards of accuracy.

Physical Activities and Working Conditions: Work is light, requiring infrequent stooping and crouching, and is performed inside. Lifting and carrying test equipment weighing 5 to 10 pounds.

Salary: Average ranges between $690 to $1,090 per month.

CHAPTER 4

EDUCATION AND TRAINING

AT THIS POINT you have some idea of the educational and training requirements for the various occupations in edp. It is obvious that a career in edp requires education and training. There is no short cut, or easy substitute. Without exception, every job requires a high school diploma. And to move up the ladder successfully, which is everyone's goal, you'll need additional education and training. Just how much depends on how far up you want to go.

If you're interested in research, design, or development of computer systems and software, you'll need at least a bachelor's degree and more likely a master's degree or doctorate in science, mathematics, or engineering. Applications and system engineering careers likewise require advanced degrees.

Those planning to enter administration, marketing, public relations, and advertising will find advanced degrees in management, business, finance, and the communication arts exceedingly helpful, and many times necessary, for advancement. Salesmen who specialize in engineering or scientific applications, usually require a technical degree; while salesmen who specialize in business applications, find a degree in business administration almost mandatory. And for the better paying positions in maintenance and service engineering, a bachelor's degree is a must. While a degree is necessary for systems analysis, programers can get by with only a high school diploma. However, programers will find their advancement limited without a degree. A degree is not required for entry level positions in computer, peripheral equipment, and keypunch operations, or for electronic technicians. Part-time college courses are needed, though, for advancement.

Years ago, when edp was in its infancy, edp instruction and training was difficult to obtain. Your learning was obtained either from the computer manufacturer, or on the job from your employer. Today, the picture has changed completely. Courses are offered in high school, college, technical trade school, and through correspondence. Many of these places even have their own computers to provide you with actual experience.

In this chapter, we'll explore the type of educational and training facilities available, and what they offer.

HIGH SCHOOLS

MANY HIGH SCHOOLS offer beginning courses in computer mathematics or Boolean algebra. Some even have computer terminals in the classroom to enable students to learn basic programing. If the school is large enough or is part of a large school system, a computer may be used to schedule classes, process grades, and handle other administrative tasks. These computers are frequently made available to students either for scheduled courses, or for extracurricular instruction. Many times the operation of the computer is turned over to the school's business department, which supervises the creation of programs or projects by students. This affords students the opportunity to acquire hands-on experience and familiarity with edp.

An excellent introduction to edp, offered in high schools, is sponsored by one of the professional edp societies (the Data Processing Management Association, see Chapter 7). Known as Future Data Processors (FDP), the course attempts 1) to stimulate interest in the many facets of edp among young people, 2) to introduce a challenging and rewarding new career, and 3) to emphasize the increasing importance of edp in the development of effective business, engineering, and public service. The heart of the FDP program is the presentation of a series of extracurricular classes, often organized as clubs, and taught by qualified instructors. Field trips are made to various edp installations.

For information on the activities available at your school, check with your school's vocational guidance counselor. He is in a position to guide your future training, advise you as to what courses are available, and in some cases even get an extracurricular job for you in some industrial installation. He will also be able to write for more information on the FDP program.

JUNIOR/COMMUNITY COLLEGES

JUNIOR OR COMMUNITY COLLEGES, also called two-year colleges, offer several good features for high school graduates. Students who are denied entrance to regular colleges due to overcrowding can continue their academic training for two years, then transfer into a regular college in the third year to finish a four-year degree course. Instruction is generally college-level. In addition, many junior colleges are vocationally oriented; they provide specialized instruction designed to gain entry level positions in the computer field. For the convenience of those holding jobs, classes can be scheduled at night or on Saturday, or all in the morning or afternoon. Also, tuition costs are lower, and many institutions permit a student to take as few courses as he desires.

Many junior colleges offer associate degrees and/or courses in data processing and programing. Some offer the uniform two-year curriculum developed by the U.S. Office of Education, which is designed to teach the business applications of edp. Graduates of this program can apply programing techniques to specific problems with a minimum of supervision. A laboratory-type course is assigned each student in his final semester; he undertakes a major application project involving analysis, design, and programing.

Appendix B lists most of the junior colleges offering degrees or courses in either the computer sciences or business data processing. Computer science is involved with the technical end of computers, while business data processing involves the use of computers in business or commercial applications. If you are interested in a junior college not listed in Appendix B, a letter to the school's registrar will bring a catalog of courses by return mail.

COLLEGES

IF YOU'RE INTERESTED in advancing in edp and establishing a solid career, you should seriously plan on a college education. There is just no substitute for it. Our colleges and universities are also increasingly aware of this need, and are steadily increasing the number and types of edp courses they offer. Hundreds of schools throughout the country offer programs in the computer sciences and business data processing. A portion of these, in addition, offer degrees in both areas. Computer science deals with mathematics, engineering, and language development; business data processing deals with commercial and financial systems. Many universities offer edp courses as part of other degree programs. These courses will be taught in schools of engineering, business, and mathematics; and deal with the application of computers in accounting and business, mathematical techniques for solving problems by computer, the use of computers in engineering, the design of computer circuits, and logic. Computing laboratories are evident in many colleges and universities. Here, students and faculty can apply course work, or undertake research in many areas of edp. Students, especially, benefit from this direct involvement with computers.

Appendix B lists colleges and universities which offer instruction and/or degrees in edp. While we have tried to make this listing as complete as possible, it is difficult to keep pace with the increasing number of institutions that are adding computer courses and degrees to their curricula. If you are interested in a college or university which is not mentioned, or in learning more about the program of one that is mentioned, write a letter to the registrar requesting information. He'll be happy to send it to you.

PRIVATE EDP SCHOOLS

PRIVATE EDP SCHOOLS, which are run for profit, are also known as business colleges, technical schools, computer schools, and programer schools. Many of these schools do a fine job, providing good instruction, hands-on experience, and concern for the student. An equal number are dishonest, provide poor instruction, and are only after your money. You will learn in this section how to distinguish between the two.

Private schools do not grant degrees (including the associate degree); generally do not schedule instruction on a semester basis; and usually limit themselves to entry level instruction in operations, servicing, or programing. They will accept both high school graduates and nongraduates. The good schools, while never promising guaranteed placement, will have active and efficient placement services that make an honest effort to get jobs for their graduates. Private schools arrange their classroom hours for the benefit of working people, scheduling a large number of evening and Saturday classes.

Tuition costs vary greatly from school to school. Courses in keypunching should cost between $125 and $200 for approximately 50 to 80 hours of instruction. A course in computer operations should run between $300 and $600. A course in computer servicing or electronics should cost between $600 to $1100. A course in beginning programing will cost between $500 to $1700, and provide anywhere from 300 to 900 hours of instruction.

Is a private school for you? That depends on what your goals are. If you do not plan to continue your education beyond high school; if you have been away from school for some years; if you understand you'll receive only *vocational* training; if you understand you'll have to start at the bottom in whatever job you take; if you understand that the school cannot guarantee you a job; if you're learning programing, and the language studied will be accepted by a prospective employer; if you understand that this training will give you no advantage over other trained job applicants; then a private school is for you.

SELECTING A PRIVATE SCHOOL

A THOROUGH INVESTIGATION and evaluation should be made of any private school you plan to attend. Several groups have produced procedures or guidelines for doing this. The best is issued by the Data Processing Management Association (see Chapter 7), and is called, *Guidelines for the Operations of Private Data Processing Educational Institutions*; it costs $1.50. Another is the *Guidelines for Data Processing Schools,* issued free by the Association for Computing Machinery (see Chapter 7). While you can obtain these documents yourself, they are written primarily for professional educators. Your school guidance counselor should have copies on file.

Informal evaluating procedures have also been issued by the American Federation of Information Processing Societies (see Chapter 7); the Better Business Bureau of Metropolitan New York, 220 Church Street, New York, N.Y. 10013; and the National Better Business Bureau, 230 Park Avenue, New York, N.Y. 10017. A nominal charge for postage and handling is made for the last two.

However, the information from the five sources mentioned, plus others, has been compiled and summarized for you below.

1. *Do not rush* into anything. *Do not sign* anything until you have checked the school's credentials and are convinced the school is reputable and you can profit from it. By-pass any school that tries to pressure you to sign a contract immediately.

2. Investigate about *five or six* schools before you decide to enroll in one. Limiting yourself to checking only one makes evaluation difficult. Reputable schools welcome comparison to others. Compare hours of instruction, costs, the school's equipment. Are texts provided? Be sure there are no "extras."

A computer operator working the console controls of an
IBM System 360/65 computer system. Tape units are visible in the background.

3. Check with your *local* Better Business Bureau or Chamber of Commerce to see if any complaints have been issued against the school, and the nature of the complaints.

4. Try to learn how long the school has been in existence. The more years the better.

5. Check with employers of edp personnel in your area. Determine their job openings, requirements, and if they are hiring graduates from the school in question. See if they feel the school provided the kind of training they needed.

6. Beware of extravagant claims made in ads, or high-pressure salesmen who claim to be "career counselors" or "guidance counselors." Avoid schools which offer you inducements such as scholarships. If the school claims to be associated with any manufacturer, demand proof, or call the manufacturer's nearest local office to check. The school may only be using equipment purchased from the manufacturer.

7. Beware of blind ads; the school's *name* and *address* should appear in the ad so you can go to see what the school looks like.

8. Absolutely avoid any school which guarantees jobs, or promises you will be something more than a trainee after graduation.

9. Is the school approved by a state agency? Though not all states require approval, write to your state's Department of Education to check.

10. Is the school accredited by at least one of the two national accrediting commissions recognized by the U.S. Office of Education? The school's literature or ads should state whether it subscribes to the National Association of Trade and Technical Schools, 2021 L St., N.W., Washington, D.C. 20036; or The Accrediting Commission for Business Schools, Suite 401, 1730 M St., N.W., Washington, D.C. 20036. Also, is the school ap-

proved by the Veterans Administration for training under the G.I. bill; or by the U.S. Department of Justice's Immigration and Naturalization Service for the training of foreign students?

11. Ask for the names and addresses of graduates of the school in your community. Any reputable school will gladly furnish these, and you should not be afraid or embarrassed to request such information. Contact these graduates and see what they think of the course, the equipment, the instruction, and so on.

12. When you visit the school, make sure the equipment you'll train on is visible. If there is no equipment around, run for the nearest exist. Disregard claims that the computer is in another building, or on another floor, is being repaired, has been ordered, or is being rented from another source.

13. Check on the backgrounds of the school's instructors. Have they had practical experience? Are they now working at computer jobs in addition to teaching? Much of this information should be included in the school's brochures and course catalogs.

14. Almost all schools give prospective students an aptitude test to see if the student has ability in his area of interest. The top-notch schools give a comprehensive, standardized admissions type such as the IBM programer's test. Beware the "specially designed" test, or one that is graded by the salesman. It should be of the self-grading type, which is designed to show you your score without the possibility of fraudulent scoring as a lure to enrollment. If you are now in high school, your vocational guidance counselor will be glad to work with you to learn your aptitudes and help guide your career. He can obtain valid aptitude tests and administer them to you independently, and grade them impartially.

15. Read all contracts *before* you sign them. Make sure the school's schedule of payments, tuition refund policy, and clauses

covering cancellation are clearly spelled out. If necessary, obtain outside assistance in reviewing the contract.

16. Does the school have at least one person devoting his full time to placement? While no school can guarantee placement, the better schools make an honest attempt at it.

If you follow the guidelines listed, and answer the questions posed to your satisfaction, you can be fairly certain the school is qualified and reputable.

ADULT EDUCATION PROGRAMS

MANY PUBLIC SCHOOL SYSTEMS, colleges, and universities offer adult education programs in the evening or on Saturday. While all types of courses are presented, the majority of the courses are vocationally oriented and are taught free or at nominal cost (up to $25). In larger cities, these courses will also be offered by trade unions, professional or fraternal groups, churches, veterans groups, and private educational organizations. The cost will be somewhat higher if the sponsoring organization is not publicly funded.

You will find many good computer courses being taught in these facilities and as the demand increases, more and more being offered. The courses are usually on a par with those offered by private edp schools, plus the cost is much less. Don't expect to find advanced instruction in mathematics or engineering in these adult education programs. But in them, as in reputable private schools, you can obtain good instruction in the fundamentals of operation and programing, which will prepare you for entry level positions in these areas.

To inquire about these adult education programs, check with your local high school, the state university, area colleges, neighborhood libraries, and local chapters of national computer associations and societies. While these organizations may not conduct classes themselves, they usually have knowledge of where the classes are taught. Your telephone directory will prove invaluable in this search.

MANUFACTURER/SERVICE COMPANY SCHOOLS

COMPUTER MANUFACTURERS and companies providing software, analysis, and other services offer some of the best instruction available. The programs are of two types: training provided with the purchase of equipment, and training provided by a manufacturer-owned or service company-owned private edp school charging tuition. In the first type, if an employer purchases new equipment or is presently using a computer system, he is allowed to send his employees to the manufacturer's school. Of course, the employer has paid for the schooling as part of the original purchase price of the computer system, but the employee/student pays nothing. The training is excellent because the student works on the latest equipment and is taught the newest techniques. Nor is a student limited to basic operating instruction. He can take advanced courses and learn about other equipment. The major computer manufacturers maintain training facilities in many large cities; in the smaller cities, manufacturers will send their training representatives directly to the user's facilities. To avail yourself of this first type of training, you must be employed by the equipment user, although you can be newly hired.

The second type of training is similar to that of the private edp school, except the school is a division or subsidiary of the manufacturer or service company. However, first-rate equipment is more the rule here than the exception, especially if the school is owned by a manufacturer. If the school is owned by a service company, students benefit in another way. Frequently, instructors will be drawn from the service company, or will be affiliated with it in various projects, helping to increase the training and education of the instructors, and to bring current practices to the classroom.

Control Data Institutes is typical of these schools. Owned by Control Data Corp., a manufacturer of large computer systems, the school offers advanced training to experienced programers as well as selected students with no previous programing background. The standard entrance requirement is completion of a programer training course, or two years of related experience, or two years of post high school education. Aptitude tests are given to each student before admission to provide an indication of his potential for success in the course offered. Training is built around a full-scale computer system with a complete complement of peripheral equipment. Half-day scheduling of classes allows the student to hold part-time work, while a student in the evening program can continue full-time employment.

These schools are generally found in or near large cities, and in or near the manufacturer's or service company's corporate headquarters. You can learn of the schools in your area by writing to the major computer manufacturers and service companies. Also, these schools will frequently be listed in the yellow pages of your telephone directory.

CORRESPONDENCE OR HOME STUDY SCHOOLS

CORRESPONDENCE or home study courses appeal to those who can't find suitable instruction locally, or who wish to study at their own pace. Usually the student is sent a text and other course material which he studies at home. At specific intervals he completes work and/or tests which are sent to the school for grading. Some schools use tape recorded instruction; others require attendance at the school during the last portion of the student's training. The one serious drawback of the majority of the schools is that they provide no means for the student to work on actual equipment. For this reason, we would recommend them only for basic or general edp instruction, or for learning a specific subject just to increase one's knowledge. A case in point would be Boolean algebra or binary arithmetic (a computer numbering system based on 2s).

Correspondence courses are offered by many private schools and colleges and universities. Private schools, like other businesses, have to make a profit. They charge between $250 to $600 for a course that will take 12 to 18 months to complete, although you can proceed more slowly. Colleges and universities, because they are supported by pubic taxes, charge only a nominal fee. Private schools sometimes employ salesmen; public institutions don't. Most private schools have placement services, but they are generally ineffective. Private schools are accredited by the National Home Study Council, 1601 Eighteenth St., N.W., Washington, D.C. 20009, which has been approved by the U.S. Office of Education. To be accredited a school must meet a number of standards, including a minimum of five years in existence.

As with private edp schools, private correspondence schools should be evaluated thoroughly. You should apply the same guidelines outlined for private edp schools to private correspondence schools, except in instances where the guidelines would not be applicable. Write to several schools for information, so you can compare costs, length of instruction, specific courses offered, and so on. Your guidance counselor will be glad to assist you in this evaluation.

Appendix C is a list of private correspondence schools offering edp instruction, and some universities which are known to offer similar instruction. The National Home Study Council will send you its latest catalog listing additional courses or changes which may occur after publication of this book. A letter of inquiry to your local college or university will bring you details of that school's program. The letter should be addressed to the Director, Correspondence Instruction, Extension Division.

ARMED SERVICES SCHOOLS

IF YOU FACE the likelihood of being drafted, of serving in a reserve status, or if you decide on a career in the Armed Services, you can take advantage of several educational opportunities being offered. Computers play as big a role in our defense structure as they do in our civilian pursuits. Computers fire and guide our missiles and guns, navigate our planes and ships, provide a means to encode our messages and decode our enemy's messages, prepare payrolls, maintain personnel records, handle inventory, prepare and maintain purchasing records, and help in a hundred other ways. Some of the biggest computer installations in existence are operated by the Army and Navy.

Because of the need for trained people to program and operate these thousands of computers in use, the services maintain many special schools and conduct on-the-job training programs to produce qualified personnel. These schools provide excellent instruction that would cost a great deal of money to obtain elsewhere.

Many service occupations are identical to civilian occupations. A recruiting officer can apprise you of the various edp occupations you can pursue and the types of education and training available.

In addition, the Armed Services maintain an excellent correspondence program that is available to any serviceman or woman. Called USAFI (United States Armed Forces Institute), it provides a large number and variety of courses. You may be interested in two relatively new courses added by USAFI—*Introduction to Data Processing,* an introductory college course; and *Computer Science,* a technical course. USAFI also offers college correspondence courses through programs in 47 colleges and universities. Approximately 10 universities are presently offering edp courses covering basic computer principles, edp operations, and programing. You can obtain more information about USAFI by writing to the Director, U.S. Armed Forces Institute, Madison, Wis. 53703.

CHAPTER 5

HOW TO GET STARTED

APTITUDE TESTS

IF YOU ARE SERIOUSLY CONSIDERING a career in edp, your first step will be to learn about and take one or more aptitude tests. While they should not be relied upon 100 percent, and need to be coupled with sound, experienced vocational guidance, they are important for two reasons—they will help determine where your vocational interests and aptitudes lie, and they are used rather widely in the selecting and hiring of many computer personnel. Aptitude tests are different from those you are normally accustomed to because they measure your ability to *think* and *demonstrate your own aptitudes,* rather than your ability to *remember* or *memorize* such as a history test might.

The aptitude tests which help reveal your vocational interests and aptitudes are general in nature and cover a wider area of subject matter than the aptitude tests used for selecting and hiring computer personnel, which are usually designed for a

specific occupation. The general aptitude tests, which are administered by your school's guidance counselor or specially qualified
psychologist working for your school system, are designed to tell
you whether you should go into law, engineering, writing,
teaching, medicine, edp, or any number of other fields. Years
ago, when vocational testing wasn't as well known or readily
available, students entered law when they should have become
engineers, or studied chemistry when they should have studied
writing, or became salesmen when they should have acquired a
degree in music or fine arts. Today, however, every student,
without hesitation, should avail himself of testing services. They
will help prevent many future heartaches and problems.

Aptitude tests are also used by employers to select personnel
in many edp occupations—usually those concerned with systems
analysis, programing, computer operation, keypunching and
data input preparation, and computer servicing and maintenance.
Private edp schools also use tests to determine whether or not a
prospective student has an aptitude for an edp career, but
frequently these tests are designed simply so that everyone will
score high in them.

Once you've taken a general aptitude test, and determined
that you have ability for and an interest in an edp career, you
will profit by familiarizing yourself with specific occupational
aptitude tests. You'll learn what to expect when you go on job
interviews, and you'll be able to gauge your present understanding and future improvement Taking these specific tests is
beneficial even if your particular specialty is one that is not
subject to testing—such as computer design, marketing, education, etc. You'll get a feel for the aptitude requirements of
related positions, and you'll get a feel for the test itself, should
a prospective employer test your aptitudes in another specialty
to see the depth of your background. For example, a salesman

who understands systems analysis or programing is an asset to any organization.

Stories are constantly being told of individuals who were nervous or frightened of taking tests for employment, even though they were qualified. Each prepared himself, though, by applying for admission to several commercial computer schools weeks before his employment interview. Each school gave a different, but similar test. The effect was to fortify the job applicant's confidence and permit him to score high on his employment test.

More tests are given for programers and systems analysts than any other. The most widely used and copied is the IBM Programer Aptitude Test. It is estimated that the test has been given to 85 percent of prospective programers. The test is actually three subtests in a single reusable booklet: a number series test, a figure analogies test, and an arithmetical reasoning test. The number series test contains 40 questions and has a 10-minute time limit. The figure analogies test contains 30 questions and has a 15-minute time limit. The arithmetical reasoning test contains 25 questions and has a 30-minute time limit. The complete test, which costs approximately $2, is available from any IBM branch office. However, not everyone can walk in off the street and purchase it. IBM logically restricts its sale to employer/users of edp equipment, reputable schools, vocational guidance counselors, and others who have a legitimate use for it.

Other widely used tests are the NCR Programing Aptitude Test, the Univac Computer Programer Aptitude Test, the Science Research Associates (SRA, an IBM subsidiary) Computer Programing Aptitude Battery, the Brandon Applied Systems Aptitude Assessment Battery-Programing, the Electronic Computer Programing Institute Data Processing Aptitude Test, the Programing Specialists, Inc. Aptitude Assessment Battery-Programing, and many others which only lack of space prevents our listing.

The NCR test is administered exclusively by NCR. The test is not for sale. Both NCR personnel and/or applicants of NCR customers are eligible to take this three-hour test.

The Univac test is somewhat different in that it tests additionally for sales ability. The test is divided into four parts: mathematical symbols, verbal analogies, mathematical reasoning, and sales attitudes. A specific time is allotted each section. The test can be obtained at Univac branch offices for a small charge.

The SRA test is also subdivided, consisting of five parts in a single reusable booklet. The sections are: verbal meanings, number approximations, letter series, reasoning, and diagraming. Time allowed is 75 minutes. It is available from SRA, 259 E. Erie St., Chicago, Ill. 60611 for approximately $6.

The Brandon test contains five problems. Each requires the ability to understand complex instructions, reason with symbols, understand statements without the aid of illustrations, and to find answers with simple calculations. No time limit is set. The test, a guide to its use, and scoring and evaluation instructions are available for approximately $6.50 from Brandon Applied Systems, 1700 Broadway, New York, N.Y. 10019.

While tests are helpful in determining ability, they should not be relied upon exclusively. Scoring high is not an indication of assured success, while scoring low may be due to factors other than ability. Ask your guidance counselor to obtain some tests and administer them to you. Also, many commercial computer schools may invite you to take their free tests. One of the best of these tests is given by Electronic Computer Programing Institute (ECPI). If you find it difficult to have a test administered to you, try to obtain the book *Computer Programer,* by Milton Luftig. It contains many samples of various computer aptitude tests, along with special sections on mathematics and pattern analysis—the material of which aptitude tests are constructed. The book sells for $5 and is published by ARCO, 219 Park Avenue South, New York, N.Y. 10003.

The U.S. Employment Service has several tests for which your vocational guidance counselor can get you scheduled. Or, if he is unable to, contact the local office of your state or U.S. Employment Service. These tests are Computer Operator, Specific Aptitude Test Battery B-565; Computer Electronics Mechanic, Specific Aptitude Test Battery B-359; Keypunch Operator, Specific Aptitude Test Battery B-499; Engineering and Scientific Programer, Specific Aptitude Test Battery B-545; and Business Edp Systems Analyst, Specific Aptitude Test Battery B-558.

HIGH SCHOOL ACTIVITIES

AFTER YOU'VE TAKEN APTITUDE TESTS, you should involve yourself in as many activities as are available in your high school. These can be regularly scheduled classes for which you'll obtain academic credit, or extracurricular activities such as clubs or special instruction.

A special kit on starting computer clubs in high school is available from the Association for Educational Data Systems, 1201 Sixteenth St., N.W., Washington, D.C. 20036. The information kit costs $1.00, and is designed to provide suggestions, materials, and encouragement to students interested in exploring computer science. A booklet within the kit contains a definition of a computer club, a statement of objectives, duties of the sponsor, and suggested activities. The kit also contains two chart articles, "What is a Computer," and "Programing";

practice problems, a bibliography, and a proposed constitution for clubs.

Another good program is the Data Processing Management Association's Future Data Processors (FDP), which was explained in Chapter 4.

Chapter 7 is a listing and description of the many technical and professional societies and organizations in edp. Check with them to see which have student chapters or other programs for you. Many of them will send you literature on a variety of subjects.

OTHER THINGS TO DO

YOU SHOULD TRY TO LEARN as much as possible about edp on your own. Write to the manufacturers for literature; their addresses are given in Appendix A. Try to obtain copies of national trade publications (see Appendix A). Major public libraries usually have copies of these publications. If possible, attend trade shows and conventions. They offer unlimited possibilities for obtaining information and literature. Try to read as many books on edp as possible. The bibliography in Appendix A is a good start.

Discuss the direction your career should take with as many knowledgeable people as possible. These would include your vocational guidance counselor, one or more of your high school teachers, local members of technical and professional societies, manufacturer's employment representatives, personnel at computer centers, and area employers of computer personnel—if you can make their acquaintances. Once you have decided in which general area of edp you wish to concentrate, you can begin your career.

GETTING AN EDUCATION

IF YOU ARE INTERESTED in anything other than operational positions such as keypunching, data typing, and so on, you will need a good education—and the more you have, the better off you are. No one should settle for less than a college education. However, if you lack finances, can't borrow the money or get a scholarship, or can't afford the four years required, you'll have to consider a junior college or other school. Having made your determination, get as much information as possible. You can write colleges for catalogs and compare their various programs, or you can make an appointment to visit their facilities and talk with the dean of the college or the registrar. You can do the same with junior colleges and private schools. Don't make hasty decisions. Weigh alternatives closely, and try to consider things as they will affect you in the long range.

GETTING A JOB

IF PERSONAL CIRCUMSTANCES do not permit further education, work with your vocational guidance counselor or school's placement officer to get a job. It is difficult at times just getting any job, but, if possible, try to land something that offers training and some future goal you can attain. The bigger companies are better in this respect. Because they employ more people, they try to maintain a training program, and can afford to have a certain percentage of trainees. You will have to carry your end, too. This usually means study on your part or attending some outside school in the evening or on Saturday. Chapter 6 discusses sources of jobs.

CHAPTER 6

SOURCES OF JOBS

SEEKING EMPLOYMENT should not be a hit-or-miss effort, but should be a well-thought-out and planned campaign. Every source should be investigated for information on prospective employers. You can compile a list of these leads arranged in order of your preferences by product or service, size of company, location, or any other considerations important to you. Every lead should be explored by phone or letter. Try to get an interview with the personnel director or person in charge of the edp facility. If there are no openings at present, leave an application or résumé on file. A job seeker must adopt the philosophy of the salesman—the more sales calls you make, the more chances you'll have to sell your product. In your case, the product is you.

THE BASIC SOURCES

PLACEMENT SERVICES are available in many high schools; in most junior colleges, colleges, and universities; and

92

in some private schools. On the high school level they provide a source of available positions, and a means for getting an introduction to an employer. On the higher educational levels they provide a means for channeling trained people into the job market. Guidance counselors usually act as placement officers in high school, while a full-time staff and a separate office is usually allotted for this service on the college level.

Another free placement service is provided by your state. Known as the State Employment Service, or State Employment Bureau, or Bureau of Employment Security, it is in the business of seeking and listing job openings, and directing qualified people to fill them. It is listed in the phone book.

Local newspapers are another source of available jobs. By checking their daily and Sunday want ad sections, you can learn of openings and get a feel for prevailing salaries, experience requirements, and types of equipment in service.

Employment agencies charge a fee for their service which is paid by either the employer or you. In theory, employment agencies save the employer time and money by screening unqualified applicants, seeking qualified people to fill job openings, and finding employers for applicants who are registered with the agency. In practice, many employment agencies do little screening. They try to force unqualified people on an employer, and they try to sell an applicant on an employer that the applicant doesn't want. Unfortunately, it is difficult to evaluate beforehand which employment agencies do a good job and earn their fee, and which provide little service except to their own bank accounts. In larger cities, some employment agencies will specialize in the placement of edp personnel. They are generally listed in the yellow pages with other employment agencies, but they will indicate their specialization.

USING YOUR OWN INITIATIVE

START WITH THE major manufacturers of computer systems. Their addresses are listed in Appendix A. If you live close to where their headquarters are located, your task is easier. Even if you are fairly distant, you many wish to relocate in the headquarters area. However, if you do not want to relocate, these systems developers do have manufacturing, service, and sales facilities throughout the country. Write or contact their branch offices. Your local phone directory is an excellent aid in this venture, or you can consult one of the industry directories listed at the end of this chapter.

Try the smaller manufacturers—companies which make small computer systems (known as minicomputers), peripheral or auxiliary equipment, and supplies. Like the major manufacturers, these smaller ones also have national and branch offices. The yellow pages phone directory will prove invaluable here. It will have a section titled "Data Processing Systems, Equipment, and Supplies," which will list the company offices in your area. A great deal of patience will be required on your part. The majority of the listings in the yellow pages are those of sales offices and representatives of the company in question. If this information is revealed when you call, merely ask if the company has a facility nearby and/or where the company's nearest personnel office is. More information than is given in the phone directory can be found in one of the industry directories listed at the end of this chapter.

Software and service companies are also a good bet for employment. There are large organizations which have national and branch offices, and smaller organizations which can have as few as one or two employees. They are listed in the yellow pages under "Data Processing Service." Here too, patience is a virtue. You will have no way of separating the wheat from the chaff beforehand; that is, of separating the sales representatives and the one-man companies from the people doing the hiring. Even using the industry directories previously mentioned will require work on your part. But when you consider you are searching for entry to a lifetime career, this is a small price to pay.

The largest source for jobs is private industry. Try large department stores, public utilities, railroads, airlines, trucking concerns, nonprofit organizations, insurance firms, banks, manufacturers of all kinds (autos, drugs, paper, food, electronics, cosmetics, etc.), large publishing houses, oil companies, and so on. Your local Chamber of Commerce can supply you with a list of the area's major companies. Check to see which have computer installations, then contact their personnel people. Be prepared for many turndowns, but don't despair or give up.

You may also find computer centers in many hospitals, colleges and universities, scientific laboratories, libraries, and credit card bureaus.

It may surprise you to know that the largest single user of edp equipment is our own federal government. It has some 5,000 computer systems operating throughout the country for the Department of Defense, Internal Revenue Service, Department of Commerce, Department of Agriculture, Atomic Energy Commission, Department of Transportation, Federal Communications Commission, Federal Trade Commission, Department of Health, Education, and Welfare, National Aeronautics and Space Administration, and many, many other departments, bureaus, and commissions. Periodically, civil service examinations are held for the many diverse job openings available. Literature announcing job requirements, salary, date of examination, and other details is yours for the asking. The federal government's personnel department is called the Civil Service Commission, and it is this agency which issues the announcements of examinations. It is always better to visit the local office of the Civil Service Commission, where you will be able to talk to someone. If that is not possible, write to the United States Civil Service Commission, 1900 E St., N.W., Washington, D.C. 20415, requesting announcements for specific edp occupations.

Don't overlook possibilities with your local or state government. Many fine computer centers are functioning for city police departments, state highway departments, bureaus of licensing and inspection, payroll departments, and others. Most city and state personnel are selected by examination under civil service procedures, but many are appointed by department heads.

INDUSTRY DIRECTORIES

THERE ARE ABOUT a dozen directories of organizations in edp which are published primarily as buyers' guides or reference sources. Though they are *not* designed as listings of job sources, you can use them as such if you are willing to do a little work and spend some time and money for phone calls and postage.

Basically, these directories contain the following information: organizations selling edp products and services; their addresses, phone numbers, and management officers; characteristics of their products and services; and their local offices and sales representatives. Many of the company listings, perhaps even a majority, may be one-man operations, and hence have no need for additional employees.

How, then, can you use these directories? First, determine which organizations are located in your vicinity or have branch offices there. Next, try to learn something about the firm from its listing. How many people does it employ? Is management limited to one man, or are there half a dozen or more people listed? Is there a marketing or sales director? This is a tip-off that the company is involved in an active production and marketing operation. Finally, cross-check your information with the yellow pages phone directory. Sales representatives will not usually be listed in the yellow pages, while local offices will be. When you've determined which firms are your prospects, you can call or write them to see if they are employers, and if they have any openings. With first-class postage now costing eight cents, it is almost as cheap to phone. If you have more time, try to visit the firm. You will make a better impression, and learn more about the organization.

If you can avoid buying these directories, so much the better. You will have little use for them at this point in your career. Try to get your guidance counselor to get them for the school, or see if any local libraries may have them. You may know someone who works in a computer center, and he may have access to one or more directories.

Here are some that may prove helpful.

Computer Directory and Buyers' Guide, published by the monthly trade publication *Computers and Automation* as a supplement to one of its summer issues. Price is $14.50; orders can be sent to Computers and Automation, 815 Washington St., Newtonville, Mass. 02160. While there is much to interest you in this directory, you will be interested particularly in the section titled, "Main Roster of Organizations in Computers and Data Processing."

Annual Reference Guide, published by the monthly trade publication *Business Automation* as its regular September issue. Check on availability and price from Business Automation, Hitchcock Bldg., Wheaton, Ill. 60187. Various sections of this directory are helpful, including the "Listing of Manufacturers and Suppliers."

Computer Industry Annual, published by the monthly trade publication *Computer Design.* Price is $10; orders can be sent to Computer Industry Annual, Box 258, West Concord, Mass. 01781. You will be interested only in the last section, "Manufacturers' Directory." Disregard all the entries listed under each manufacturer, as they refer to the firm's sales and service representatives.

World Directory of Computer Companies, published by Computer and Technology Information, Inc., 500 Newport Center Dr., Newport Beach, Calif. 92660. Price is approximately $15.

Computer Industry Guide, published by Resource Publications Inc., 194 Nassau St., Princeton, N.J. 08540. Price is $6.95. This is a somewhat dated directory, having been published in August 1969. Also, the directory seems to be a compilation of company-originated advertising and public relations information. However, it does have a "Career Opportunities" section which has profiles on approximately 40 companies.

The International Directory of Computer and Information System Services, published by Europa Publications Ltd., 18 Bedford Sq., London, W.C.1. Price is $15. This directory is somewhat dated, too, being published in March 1969. Though it is a worldwide compilation, approximately 100 pages are devoted to American firms. If this directory is available in a library for consultation, it will be helpful. However, for your purposes, it is not worth purchasing.

Directory of Data Processing Service Centers, published by the trade organization Association of Data Processing Service Organizations, 420 Lexington Ave., New York, N.Y. 10017. Issued free to members and customers, this directory lists all the

A terminal system is needed when the user is located some distance from the computer, or when the user desires to transmit information to or receive information from a remote point as much as thousands of miles away. In the IBM 2770 terminal system shown here, the operator has learned to use the card reader (upper right), the display station (center), and the medium-speed serial printer (foreground).

members of the association, and is a good guide to prospective employers.

Directory of the Computer Industry in the Washington, D.C. Area, published by Applied Library Resources, 3801 N. Fairfax Dr., Suite 50, Arlington, Va. 22203. Price is $6.95. Some useful information is contained in this directory. There are, however, a number of listings which lack sufficient information, and a number of listings of government facilities which can only hire through civil service.

Computers 70, published by KHL Associates, 552 Mission St., San Francisco, Calif. 94105. Price is $10.50. This is a census of computer installations and a directory of computer service companies in the San Francisco bay area.

WEMA Directory, published by the trade group Western Electronics Manufacturers Association, 2600 El Camino Real, Palo Alto, Calif. 94306, and 3600 Wilshire Blvd., Los Angeles, Calif. 90005. Issued free to members; $15 to others. Contains both electronic and information technology (edp) industries in the West.

Official Directory of Data Processing, 444 Burchett St., Glendale, Calif. 91203. Published in two sections—Eastern USA and Western USA. Lists 25,000 edp users and 6,000 edp suppliers. Each section is priced at $22.50, or $50 for both sections.

CHAPTER 7

TECHNICAL AND PROFESSIONAL
SOCIETIES AND ORGANIZATIONS

AMERICAN FEDERATION OF INFORMATION
PROCESSING SOCIETIES (AFIPS)
210 Summit Ave., Montvale, N. J. 07645

AFIPS WAS FOUNDED in 1961 primarily to coordinate activity between several existing societies and to sponsor two annual conferences. It has grown steadily since then, attracting more societies to its fold, and undertaking research in several important areas such as manpower, job classification, and wages.

Membership in AFIPS is not direct, but rather through one of its constituent societies. These include the American Institute of Aeronautics and Astronautics (AIAA), the American Institute of Certified Public Accountants (AICPA), the American Society for Information Science (ASIS), the American Statistical Association (ASA), the Association for Computing Machinery (ACM), the Association for Computational Linguistics (ACL), the Computer Society of the Institute of Electrical and Electronics

Engineers (IEEE-CS), the Instrument Society of America (ISA), the Simulation Councils, Inc. (SCI), the Society for Industrial and Applied Mathematics (SIAM), the Society for Information Display (SID), and the Special Libraries Association (SLA).

The objectives of AFIPS are:

To advance and disseminate knowledge about the information processing societies.

To cooperate with local, national, and international organizations or agencies on matters pertaining to information processing; to serve as representatives of the United States of America in international organizations.

To promote unity and effectiveness of effort among all those who are devoting themselves to information processing by research, by application of its principles, by teaching, or by study.

To foster the relations of the sciences of information processing to other sciences and to the arts and industries.

Though AFIPS is diversifying its activities, its major emphasis continues to be sponsorship of the two most eagerly attended events in data processing each year—the spring and fall joint computer conferences. The SJCC (held in the East) and the FJCC (held in the West) attract tens of thousands of computer professionals to several days of seminars and discussions on important issues and new techniques in edp. An exhibition, which is part of each conference, gives manufacturers and service organizations an opportunity to display their newest wares.

AMERICAN SOCIETY FOR CYBERNETICS (ASC)
2121 Wisconsin Ave., N.W., Washington, D. C. 20007

CYBERNETICS IS THE STUDY of the similarity between the ways in which humans or animals act and the ways in which machines act. Cyberneticists study organic and machine processes with a view to duplicating the human nervous system and the brain with equipment devices.

Though the ASC is a smaller society than most, its members make up in dedication and activity what they lack in numbers. Some of the world's foremost scientists are members of ASC.

The society's objectives are:

To foster progress of theoretical, technical, and applied cybernetics by means of research programs, scientific conferences, and other means.

To encourage teaching and studies of cybernetics in academic and scientific research organizations.

To foster public understanding of cybernetics.

To publish and distribute papers on, and the results of, cybernetics studies and investigations.

The ASC publishes proceedings of its conferences, a newsletter, and a quarterly journal. Each year the ASC presents the Norbert Wiener Gold Medal for the most outstanding paper by an author under 35. Its Norbert Wiener Silver Medal is presented for the most outstanding paper by an author, irrespective of age. Norbert Wiener is credited with founding the science of cybernetics.

AMERICAN SOCIETY FOR INFORMATION SCIENCE (ASIS)
1140 Connecticut Ave., N.W., Washington, D. C. 20036

ASIS IS CONCERNED with the creation, organization, and application of knowledge concerning information and its transfer. Members are interested in a wide area of activities such as library and information systems, automatic indexing, the design of systems for locating and acquiring information, management of information centers, computer linguistics, microphotography, and automated language processing.

The ASIS undertakes research in information science and provides its members with several publications, a placement service, and furthers professional development and advancement. The society has an annual conference and chapters throughout the country. ASIS invites student membership.

ASSOCIATION FOR COMPUTING MACHINERY (ACM)
1133 Avenue of the Americas, New York, N. Y. 10036

THE ACM IS ONE of the largest and most active organizations within edp. Founded in 1947, the society is dedicated to the development of information processing as a science, and to the responsible use of computers. In earlier years, the society's emphasis lay in the area of software and programing languages, but today the society is active in all areas of edp.

There are a number of student chapters throughout the country, with several offering scholarships and prizes to students. The ACM publishes a monthly technical journal, *Communications of the ACM*; a monthly, *Computing Reviews*; and two quarterlies, *Computing Surveys,* and *Journal of the ACM.* The society sponsors an annual conference, regional meetings and seminars.

The objectives of the ACM are:

To advance the sciences and arts of information processing including the study, design, development, construction, and application of modern machinery, computing techniques, and appropriate languages for general information processing, for scientific computation, and for automatic control.

To promote the free interchange of information about the sciences and arts of information processing both among specialists and the public in the best scientific and professional tradition.

The concern of the ACM with the quality and performance of data processing schools led to the issuance in May 1969 of its *Guidelines for Data Processing Schools*. The intent is to provide minimal guidelines for public and private schools, for accrediting agencies and the interested public, and for guidance counselors, and prospective students. You can obtain a copy of these guidelines by sending a letter to the ACM.

ASSOCIATION OF COMPUTER PROGRAMERS AND ANALYSTS (ACPA)
2 Pennsylvania Plaza, Suite 1500, New York, N. Y. 10001

FOR YEARS, MANY PROGRAMERS and analysts felt they needed a society of their own. The larger organizations, they felt, represented too many occupational groups in edp. This belief led to the formation of the ACPA in 1970, making it the youngest and newest society in the field. The organization is dedicated to the personal advancement and greater public recogniion of the computer application profession.

There are several grades of membership, each based on a graduated scale of actual experience and qualification as a programer or analyst.

The society offers a national recruitment service, career counseling, an annual conference, seminars, workshops, and several publications.

ASSOCIATION OF DATA PROCESSING SERVICE ORGANIZATIONS (ADAPSO)
420 Lexington Ave., New York, N. Y. 10017

ADAPSO IS A TRADE ASSOCIATION of companies providing data processing services for profit. Sometimes called service bureaus or service centers, these businesses provide a wide range of computing services such as payroll preparation, billing, stock brokerage record keeping, inventory control, and so on. If you plan on opening your own business someday, you may want to investigate the benefits offered by ADAPSO membership.

The objectives of ADAPSO are:

To exchange service center management know-how for providing effective service to the business community.

To develop high performance and ethical standards among its members.

To create general public acceptance of the service bureau concept.

To provide mutual assistance to member companies.

To offer a forum for discussion of industry problems.

APAPSO sponsors three conferences each year and publishes literature pertaining to its activities.

ASSOCIATION FOR EDUCATIONAL DATA SYSTEMS (AEDS)
1201 Sixteenth St., N.W., Washington, D. C. 20036

FOUNDED IN 1962, the AEDS is concerned primarily with the use of data processing in the administrative aspects of education.

The objectives of the AEDS are:

To establish a central file of procedures and programs on data processing in education.

To organize national seminars and workshops for the advancement of educational data processing.

To provide a professional placement service.

To encourage quality publications in the field.

AEDS publishes the monthly *AEDS Monitor*, the quarterly *Journal of Educational Data Processing*, and several other publications.

ASSOCIATION FOR COMPUTATIONAL LINGUISTICS (ACL)
c/o Prof. Harry H. Josselson, Slavic Dept.,
Wayne State University, Detroit, Mich. 48202

THE ACL WAS FOUNDED IN 1962 to promote research in the translation of languages by electromechanical or automatic equipment. The society sponsors an annual meeting; in odd-numbered years held in conjunction with the Spring Joint Computer Conference, in even-numbered years held in conjunction with the Linguistic Society of America.

The ACL publishes a quarterly journal, *Mechanical Translation*, and a monthly magazine, *The Finite String*.

ASSOCIATION OF SYSTEMS MANAGEMENT (ASM)
24587 Bagley Rd., Cleveland, Ohio 44138

THE ASM IS AN ORGANIZATION of administrative executives and specialists in systems work serving business, education, and government. It is concerned with forms control, human relations, organization, procedure writing, and systems applications.

The objectives of the ASM are:

To promote and foster improved management systems and procedures through research, education, and the exchange of ideas.

To promote a broad understanding and acceptance of the systems function for effective management.

The ASM sponsors an annual Systems Man of the Year Award, and an annual international meeting. A $2,000 research grant is offered to Ph.D. candidates in the systems field. The association publishes a monthly journal, a monthly newsletter, and several other important monographs, reports, and guides.

ASSOCIATION FOR SYMBOLIC LOGIC (ASL)
P.O. Box 6248, Providence, R. I. 02904

THE ASL IS AN INTERNATIONAL ORGANIZATION for the promotion of research in, and the study of, mathematical logic. Mathematical logic is concerned with the use of mathematics to represent everyday situations and concepts. If we can reduce or translate hard to understand concepts or weighty problems into numbers, we could probably simplify the concepts or solve the problems by using the numbers in a formula or equation, and solving the equation as we do, for example, in algebra.

The ASL provides a meeting ground for mathematicians and philosophers. The society publishes a quarterly journal.

BUSINESS EQUIPMENT MANUFACTURERS ASSOCIATION (BEMA)
1828 L St., N.W., Washington, D. C. 20036

BEMA IS A TRADE ASSOCIATION of manufacturers of data processing and office equipment. It is composed of approximately 60 companies organized into three main groups dealing with data processing, office machines, and office equipment. BEMA provides the industry with a forum for discussing common problems, and by the work of its many committees and councils, a means for solving these broad problems.

The Data Processing Group of BEMA is the administrative sponsor of one of the most important committees in edp—the sectional committee on Computers and Information Processing of the American National Standards Institute. This sectional committee has the responsibility for developing national and industry-wide standards for edp. A standard is a commonly accepted or established way of doing some task, or designing some equipment, or communicating some information. We are affected every day by standards, but never give them much thought. For example, the keys of a typewriter are arranged in a precise manner by every manufacturer. Think how bad it would be if each manufacturer arranged the typewriter keyboard in a different way. We would have to learn to type on a dozen different keyboards. There are standards everywhere. Driving on the right hand side of the road is a standard. Speaking a language is a standard—each word means precisely one thing. In like manner, many standards are used in edp. Programing languages used by one group must be the same as programing languages used by another group. A reel of magnetic tape must fit machines made by all manufacturers. You can begin to see why standards are so important.

BEMA sponsors an annual business equipment exposition and conference, publishes a weekly news bulletin, and many reports of interest to the industry.

DATA PROCESSING MANAGEMENT ASSOCIATION (DPMA)
505 Busse Highway, Park Ridge, Ill. 60068

THE DPMA IS ANOTHER of the large, very active, influential organizations in edp. Founded in 1951, the organization has grown to a membership of approximately 25,000, divided into 200 chapters. Initially, DPMA was concerned with those who managed edp installations or facilities. However, as with the other groups in edp, DPMA broadened its outlook to include concern for almost all the other areas of edp.

The objectives of DPMA are:

To promote and develop inquiry in edp and data processing management.

To foster education among its members for a better understanding of the nature of edp.

To undertake research for the improvement of edp.

To make known by all appropriate means all sound edp principles and methods.

To supply to its members current information in the field of edp management, and to cooperate with them and with educational institutions in the advancement of the science of edp.

DPMA sponsors an annual conference, many regional conferences and seminars, and several programs and grants. The society publishes a monthly magazine, *Data Management*.

Concerned with the lack of standards in the teaching of edp by private edp schools and similar educational institutions, DPMA established a committee to study the problems and recommend solutions. After a year of intensive work, the committee produced a noteworthy document, *Guidelines for the Operation of Private Data Processing Educational Institutions*. This work has provided many with the necessary yardsticks which can be used to evaluate private educational institutions teaching edp.

In June 1962, DPMA established the first examination for the Certificate in Data Processing (CDP), a test for competence and ability in edp. Awarding of the Certificate was the first move by a national organization to establish professional standards. Since 1962, testing for the CDP has become an annual event at more than 50 centers in the United States and Canada.

More than 20,000 people have taken this test which is open to anyone, whether a member of DPMA or not. To be eligible, you must a) complete a prescribed course of academic study, b) have at least three years of direct work experience in a computer installation, and c) have high character qualifications. Complete information can be obtained from DPMA.

Also in 1962, DPMA embarked on a plan to offer an introductory course in edp to high school students. Called the "Future Data Processors" program, it is the most extensive voluntary secondary education program sponsored by an edp organization. Its objective is to stimulate career interest in edp, to emphasize the need for qualified individuals, and to provide information on the importance of electronic equipment for information systems. Classes are taught by representatives of local DPMA chapters. Instructor's manuals and student material are provided by DPMA.

IEEE COMPUTER SOCIETY (IEEE-CS)
8949 Reseda Blvd., Suite 202, Northridge, Calif. 91324

THIS SOCIETY IS ACTUALLY part of a much larger one—the Institute of Electrical and Electronics Engineers (IEEE). With headquarters in New York City, the IEEE represents more than 160,000 electrical and electronics engineers throughout the world. It would be difficult for one society to represent the many interests of such a large membership. Though most of the members are electronics engineers, some are concerned with television, some with spacecraft, others with radar, and so on. There are more than 20 of these special interests. It was natural, therefore, that members who wanted to concentrate in one area of electronics, or who wanted to exchange knowledge with those of similar interests, would create special interest groups. The Computer Society is one of these special interest groups. It has a membership of approximately 20,000. With the increase in newer members, the IEEE-CS is slowly changing its outlook. The younger members, fresh from college courses in the computer sciences, think of themselves as computer engineers or scientists rather than as electrical or electronics engineers.

The objectives of IEEE-CS are:

To advance the theory and practice of computer and information processing technology.

To promote the exchange of technical information among its members.

To hold meetings for the presentation and discussion of technical papers.

The IEEE-CS sponsors an annual conference, and several regional conferences. It publishes the monthly *IEEE Transactions on Computers,* and an outstanding bimonthly, *Computer.*

SIMULATION COUNCILS, INC. (SCI)
P.O. Box 2228, La Jolla, Calif. 92037

THE SCI IS A TECHNICAL SOCIETY created to advance the art and science of simulation. Simulation is a technique for building a mathematical model of a system or physical state using a computer. Modeling is an age-old technique to see what something looks like before it is built. Sculptors build a small model before they create their actual sculpture. Automobile and airplane designers build scale models before they start production on the real thing. Even architects build scale models of buildings and cities to show viewers what the actual construction will look like when completed.

It is somewhat difficult to build models of more complex things like chemical processing plants or communication network systems. It is even impossible to model some situations. For example, how can one model a spacecraft docking under actual conditions? Here is where simulation comes in. By use of a computer, we can construct a model of almost any object, system, or state. What is even better, we can make all types of alterations on the computer model to see which variations will improve the actual object or system. Obviously, simulation is a very important technique.

Because computers of all types are the main tools of the trade in simulation, the use of computers for modeling is SCI's primary concern. To improve communications among professionals in its field, SCI sponsors domestic and foreign conferences and seminars. To aid in developing simulation, SCI cooperates with other technical societies, government agencies, and educational institutions. National meetings are held in conjunction with each Joint Computer Conference. SCI publishes the monthly technical journal *Simulation.*

SOCIETY OF DATA EDUCATORS (SDE)
247 Edythe St., Livermore, Calif. 94550

THE SDE IS AN ASSOCIATION of educators interested professionally in edp. Members, if they wish, can also join one of the 10 federated societies affiliated with SDE. The society believes that teachers at all levels should be knowledgeable about automation in order to help their students develop into the best possible citizens, socially and vocationally, as far as teaching can accomplish this.

The objectives of SDE are:

To encourage all teachers to learn how automation will affect them and their students.

To provide articles for teachers that will enrich their edp backgrounds.

To provide materials that will show how others are teaching edp.

To keep teachers informed as to the research being conducted in educational edp.

To encourage students to learn about edp, particularly those who expect to teach.

To encourage schools to provide first-class instruction and impart knowledge and skill their students need for the world of tomorrow.

To encourage teachers to improve their edp teaching ability through Certificates of Proficiency, school accreditations, and the Teacher of the Year award.

SDE has been holding its international convention in conjunction with AEDS. This has been a profitable association for both; SDE stresses the instructional side of edp, while AEDS emphasizes the administrative point of view.

The society publishes a monthly magazine from October through May, the *Journal of Data Education.* Each spring this journal carries a listing of schools offering summer courses in edp. The journal solicits articles by students. SDE also publishes bulletins, newsletters, and other educational material. Student membership in SDE is invited, as is the formation of student chapters.

The following are the federated societies of SDE.

The Society for Automation in Business Education (SABE) is concerned with automation as it relates to accounting, merchandising, and commerce.

The Society for Automation in English and the Humanities

(SAEH) is interested in computer applications in English, literature, language, and philosophy.

The Society for Automation in the Fine Arts (SAFA) assists artists and educators interested in computer-generated or computer-assisted creative arts, including painting and music.

The Society for Automation in Professional Education (SAPE) is concerned primarily with the management and operation of campus computer centers for instructional purposes.

The Society for Automation in Science and Mathematics (SASM) is for those interested in astronomy, biology, chemistry, geology, mathematics, physics, medicine, and scientific edp.

The Society for Automation in the Social Sciences (SASS) is devoted to the use of edp in anthropology, economics, geography, history, political science, and sociology.

The Society for Educational Data Systems (SEDS) is concerned mainly with the administrative aspects of edp in educational institutions. It appeals to the people who manage and operate campus computer centers for such applications as class scheduling and sectioning, grade reporting, and test scoring.

Three more societies have also affiliated with SDE recently. They are the Babbage Society, the Society of Independent and Private School Data Educators, and the Society of Educational Programers and Systems Analysts. Information about these groups can be obtained from SDE.

SOCIETY FOR INDUSTRIAL AND APPLIED MATHEMATICIANS (SIAM)
33 S. 17th St., Phila., Pa. 19103

THE USUAL HOME of a mathematician is a school or university. Industrial or applied mathematicians are mathema-

One of Honeywell's regional data processing centers located in Minneapolis. A high-speed printer operator (left) checks the output of the high-speed printer. The output is being stacked in the wire basket on the floor. In the center, a data typist is recording information directly on magnetic tape, while in the background (right), a card/tape converter operator is transferring data from punch cards to magnetic tape.

ticians who leave the school or university and go into industry or science, using their skills to produce products or engage in basic research leading to products or services. SIAM is their professional organization.

SIAM, founded in 1952, has approximately 4,000 members of which about 300 are student members. The society's purpose is to promote basic research in mathematics and to provide for an exchange of information and ideas between mathematicians and other scientific personnel. SIAM publishes a bimonthly *Journal on Applied Mathematics,* a quarterly *SIAM Review,* and several other quarterlies. It sponsors an International Congress on Programing, and symposia on edp education.

SOCIETY FOR INFORMATION DISPLAY (SID)
647 N. Sepulveda Blvd., Bel Air, Los Angeles, Calif. 90049

When a computer processes data, the data is in the form of invisible electrons. To be meaningful, this data or information must be converted to some observable form—it must be displayed. The computer does this in many ways. Information can be displayed on a television picture tube, on lighted buttons or dials similar to those on your radio or hi-fi equipment, on gauges or lights similar to those on your father's automobile dashboard, and so on. In sum, whenever you see a computer with blinking panel lights, moving numbers, lighted pushbuttons, plotters, printers, and a host of other devices, you are witnessing information being displayed.

The SID, therefore, has as its objectives:

To encourage and contribute to the scientific advancement of information display.

To maintain a central file of display information for its members.

To provide forums for the exchange and distribution of ideas and knowledge concerning information display.

To establish standards and definitions in the field of information display.

To stimulate new ideas and foster their development.

SID was founded in 1963 and has approximately 2,000 members in about 10 chapters. It publishes the bimonthly *Information Display,* and sponsors an annual conference, technical meetings, and seminars.

SOCIETY FOR MANAGEMENT INFORMATION SYSTEMS (SMIS)
One First National Plaza, Chicago, Ill. 60670

SMIS IS ONE OF THE NEWEST of the edp societies. Founded in November 1968, the SMIS is concerned with the effective use of information systems for the improvement of management. The society works to improve the exchange of information between management and systems analysts and programers.

The objectives of SMIS are:

To develop efficient and productive techniques for management information systems.

To develop methods for evaluating various management information systems.

To sponsor timely programs for the presentation of new information.

The society sponsors a national conference, publishes several publications, and conducts original research. College students interested in the activities of the society are eligible for membership.

SPECIAL LIBRARIES ASSOCIATION (SLA)
235 Park Avenue South, New York, N. Y. 10003

THE SLA PROMOTES the establishment of special libraries
or information centers for specific subjects or groups, such as in
scientific, research, or manufacturing facilities. The society
encourages the use of knowledge through the collection, organization, and availability of information. The SLA also stimulates
research in the field of information services. It publishes a
monthly *Technical Book Review Index,* and several other publications. The SLA, which has about 7,000 members in approximately 35 chapters, sponsors an annual national convention, and
several sectional meetings.

APPENDIX A

SOURCES OF FURTHER INFORMATION

BY THIS TIME, you may have decided either to pursue a career in edp or to gain more detailed knowledge of the subject to help you make a decision. In either case, you need additional information. Fortunately, a wealth of sources exists. This appendix will indicate those sources. There are places to which you can write for material. There are books which can be obtained from your school or free public library.* There are even trade shows and exhibitions which you could attend, providing you live close enough. The amount of knowledge you can acquire is dependent upon only one thing—your own resourcefulness.

When writing for information, it pays to follow a few simple guidelines.

The shorter your letter, the better. The person who reads your letter may receive hundreds each day. He doesn't have time to wade through a long, rambling letter.

Be specific. Many letter writers start off with something like, "I'm not sure what I need, but I'm interested in learning as much as I can about data processing." If you don't know what you want, how can you expect someone else to know.

Don't ask for, or expect, personal replies. Most companies use printed form letters to reply to your letter. They could not afford to answer each letter individually. Also, don't ask for detailed recommendations such as, "I live in Mason City. Please tell me the best computer school there." The individual reading the letter wouldn't know. If by some chance he did know, he wouldn't say so anyway. For it would be unethical, and against his company's policy, to promote one school over another.

---

*See "Suggested Reading," on page 156.

Besides, this type of information is known better by your high school counselor, your teacher, your better business bureau, or others in your community.

Finally, be realistic in your request. Think before you write. Don't ask for things you know are unobtainable. Company librarians frequently get requests such as the following. "Please send me all the books you have on computers." To fill such a request, a librarian would have to empty her shelves of some 10,000 books.

MANUFACTURERS

Some manufacturers are an excellent source of material and are delighted to send it to you. There are eight major manufacturers. Here are their names and addresses:

Burroughs Corp., 6071 2nd Ave., Detroit, Mich. 48232
Control Data Corp. (CDC), 8100 34th Ave. S., Minneapolis, Minn. 55440
Digital Equipment Corp. (DEC), 146 Main St., Maynard, Mass. 01754
Honeywell, Inc., Information Systems, 60 Walnut St., Wellesley Hills, Mass. 02181
International Business Machines Corp. (IBM), DP Div., 1133 Westchester Ave., White Plains, N.Y. 10604
National Cash Register Co. (NCR), Main and K Sts., Dayton, Ohio 45409
UNIVAC Div., Sperry Rand Corp., P.O. Box 500, Blue Bell, Pa. 19422
Xerox Data Systems (XDS), 701 S. Aviation Blvd., El Segundo, Calif. 90245

SOCIETIES AND ORGANIZATIONS

Societies and organizations offer a rich supply of information. Chapter 7 lists specific information on technical and professional societies and trade organizations in edp. All the groups mentioned will send you information on their own programs. Some, in addition, have general information about edp which is free. Those who have general information are AFIPS, ACM, BEMA, and DPMA.

NATIONAL TRADE PUBLICATIONS

The edp industry is blessed with an abundance of trade publications. Though their content may be somewhat beyond your grasp at the moment, there are good reasons for looking through them. They will provide you with an overall view of edp, and make you aware of the many facets of the industry. Almost all the publications will send you an issue. Here are their names and addresses:

ADP Newsletter, 430 Park Ave., New York, N.Y. 10022

AEDS Journal; AEDS Monitor, 1201 16th St., N.W., Washington, D.C. 20036

ASC Newsletter, 2121 Wisconsin Ave., N.W., Washington, D.C. 20007

Automation, Penton Bldg., Cleveland, Ohio 44113

BEMA News Bulletin, 1828 L St., N.W., Washington, D.C. 20036

Burroughs Clearing House, P.O. Box 418, Detroit, Mich. 48232

Business Automation, Hitchcock Bldg., Wheaton, Ill. 60187

Communications of ACM; Computing Reviews; Computing Surveys; Data Base; Journal of ACM, 1133 Avenue of the Americas, New York, N.Y. 10036

Computer, Computer Society of IEEE, 8949 Reseda Blvd., Suite 202, Northridge, Calif. 91324

Computer Decisions, 50 Essex St., Rochelle Park, N.J. 07662

Computer Design, Professional Bldg., Baker Ave., West Concord, Mass. 01781

Computer Operations, c/o Prof. L. Harris, Pace College, 41 Park Row, New York, N.Y. 10038

Computers and Automation, 815 Washington St., Newtonville, Mass. 02160

Computers and the Humanities, Queens College, Flushing, N.Y. 11367

Computerworld, 797 Washington St., Newton, Mass. 02160

Computing Report; Data Processor, IBM Corp., 1133 Westchester Ave., White Plains, N.Y. 10604

Data Management, 505 Busse Hwy., Park Ridge, Ill. 60068

Datamation, 35 Mason St., Greenwich, Conn. 06830 (or) 94 S. Los Robles Ave., Pasadena, Calif. 91101

Data Processing Magazine, 134 N. 13th St., Philadelphia, Pa. 19107

Data Product News, 1301 Avenue of the Americas, New York, N.Y. 10019

Data Systems News, P.O. Box 7387, 200 Madison Ave., New York, N.Y. 10016

EDP Analyzer, 134 Escondido Ave., Vista, Calif. 92083
EDP Industry Report, P.O. Box 1, Newtonville, Mass. 02160
EDP Weekly, 514 10th St., N.W., Washington, D.C. 20004
Finite String; Mechanical Translation, c/o Prof. Harry M. Josselson,
   Slavic Dept., Wayne State Univ., Detroit, Mich. 48202
Honeywell Computer Journal, 60 Walnut St., Wellesley Hills, Mass.
   02181
IBM Journal of Research and Development; IBM Systems Journal, 590
   Madison Ave., New York, N.Y. 10022
Information Display, 825 S. Barrington Ave., Los Angeles, Calif. 90049
Information Retrieval and Library Automation, Lomond Systems, Inc.,
   Mt. Airy, Md. 21771
Journal of ASIS, Suite 804, 1140 Connecticut Ave., N.W., Washington,
   D.C. 20036
Journal of Data Education, San Digeo State College, San Diego, Calif.
   92115
Journal of Educational Data Processing, P.O. Box 2995, Stanford, Calif.
   94305
Journal of Systems Management, 24587 Bagley Rd., Cleveland, Ohio
   44138
Law and Computer Technology, 839 17th St., N.W., Washington, D.C.
   20006
Modern Data, 3 Lockland Ave., Framingham, Mass. 01701
Simulation, P.O. Box 2228, La Jolla, Calif. 92037
Software Age, 2211 Fordem Ave., Madison, Wis. 53701
Telecommunications, 610 Washington St., Dedham, Mass. 02026

CONFERENCES, CONVENTIONS, AND TRADE SHOWS

National conferences, conventions, and exhibitions afford
one an excellent opportunity to see the latest equipment, get
pounds and pounds of free literature, attend some seminars,
hobnob with professionals, listen to speeches, and hear endless
conversations about edp. Unfortunately, not everyone can take
advantage of conventions and conferences. Unless you live close
to where one is being held, it may be difficult, if not impossible,
to travel to the meeting site.

Almost all of the societies and organizations mentioned in
Chapter 7 hold some sort of annual get-together. If you are
interested in any group in particular, a letter to that group will

bring by return mail the date and location of that organization's next conference.

Though there are many conferences each year, with each one attracting a devoted following, about a half-dozen attract the largest number of people. They are the Spring and Fall Joint Computer Conferences sponsored by AFIPS; and the conferences and exhibitions sponsored by ACM, BEMA, DPMA, and IEEE-CS.

The list which follows contains those events for which the sites and dates have been established.

1972

SJCC	— Atlantic City, N.J.	— May 15-18
ACM	— Boston, Mass.	— August 14-16
FJCC	— Las Vegas, Nev.	— November 13-16

1973

SJCC	— Atlantic City, N.J.	— May 14-17
FJCC	— site not yet finalized; either	
	Houston, Tex.	— December 2-6
	(or)	
	Las Vegas, Nev.	— November 12-15

1974

| SJCC | — Atlantic City, N.J. | — April 29 - May 2 |
| FJCC | — Las Vegas, Nev. | — November 18-21 |

1975

| SJCC | — Atlantic City, N.J. | — May 12-15 |
| FJCC | — Las Vegas, Nev. | — November 17-20 |

1976

| SJCC | — Atlantic City, N.J. | — May 17-20 |
| FJCC | — Las Vegas, Nev. | — November 1-4 |

COMMUNITY AND JUNIOR COLLEGES, COLLEGES, AND UNIVERSITIES OFFERING COURSES AND DEGREES IN EDP

WHILE COURSES AND DEGREES in data processing may vary as to title or content, they generally tend to fall into two main groups—those dealing with mathematics, engineering, language design, etc.; and those dealing with inventory, billing, reporting, and other commercial and financial transactions. The first group is referred to as the computer sciences; the second as business data processing.

We have followed such grouping in this appendix. Thus, if one is interested in studying the technical side of computers, or in their use in technical applications, he should choose courses in the computer sciences; while one interested in the use of computers in business applications should concentrate in courses in the second group.

LEGEND: Junior or Community College = JC
Computer Sciences Courses = CS
Business Data Processing Courses = BDP
Degrees — Science = S
Business = B

ALABAMA

Auburn University
Auburn 36833
CS-BDP
Birmingham-Southern College
Birmingham 35204
BDP
Judson College
Marion 36756
BDP
Spring Hill College
Mobile 36608
BDP
University of South Alabama
Mobile 36608
BDP
Alabama College
Montevallo 35115
BDP
Huntingdon College
Montgomery 36106
BDP
Alabama State A & M Institute
Normal 35762
CS
Talladega College
Talladega 35160
CS
Troy State College
Troy 36081
BDP
Tuskegee Institute
Tuskegee 36088
CS
University of Alabama
University 35486
CS-BDP

ALASKA

University of Alaska
College 99735
CS-BDP

ARIZONA

Arizona State University
Flagstaff 86001
BDP
Arizona State College
Tempe 85281
CS-BDP-S
Eastern Arizona Jr. College
Thatcher 85552
JC-BDP
Arizona Western College
Yuma 85364
JC-BDP-B

ARKANSAS

University of Arkansas
Fayetteville 72701
CS-BDP-S
Little Rock University
Little Rock 72204
CS-BDP
Southern State College
Magnolia 71753
BDP-B
Arkansas State College
State College 72467
BDP

CALIFORNIA

Chaffey College
Alta Loma 91701
JC-BDP-B
Pacific Union College
Angwin 94508
CS-BDP
Cabrillo College
Aptos 95003
JC-BDP
Humboldt State College
Arcata 95521
CS-BDP

Azusa Pacific College
  Azusa 91702
    BDP
Citrus Jr. College
  Azusa 91702
    JC-CS-BDP
Bakersfield College
  Bakersfield 93305
    JC-BDP-B
University of California
  Berkeley 94720
    CS-BDP-S
Palo Verde Jr. College
  Blythe 92225
    JC-BDP-B
West Valley Jr. College
  Campbell 95008
    JC-CS-BDP-B
Chico State College
  Chico 95926
    CS-BDP-B
Southwestern College
  Chula Vista 92010
    JC-CS-BDP-B
Pomona College
  Claremont 91711
    CS-BDP
Harvey Mudd College
  Claremont 91711
    CS-S
Compton Jr. College
  Compton 90220
    JC-BDP-B
Orange Coast College
  Costa Mesa 92626
    JC-CS-BDP-B
University of California
  Davis 95616
    CS-S
Grossmont College
  El Cajon 92020
    JC-CS-BDP-B

El Camino College
  El Camino 90506
    JC-CS-BDP-B
Fresno Jr. College
  Fresno 93704
    JC-BDP-B
Fresno State College
  Fresno 93726
    CS-BDP-S
California State College
  Fullerton 92631
    CS-BDP
Fullerton Jr. College
  Fullerton 92631
    JC-CS-BDP-B
Gavilan College
  Gilroy 95020
    JC-CS
Glendale College
  Glendale 91208
    JC-BDP-S-B
California State College
  Hayward 94542
    CS-BDP-B
Chabot College
  Hayward 94545
    JC-BDP-B
Northrop Institute of
  Technology
    Inglewood 90306
      CS
University of California
  Irvine 92664
    CS-BDP
College of Marin
  Kentfield 94904
    JC-BDP-B
Antelope Valley Jr. College
  Lancaster 93534
    JC-BDP-B
California College of Commerce
  Long Beach 90813
    JC-CS-BDP

California State College
Long Beach 90804
CS-BDP
Long Beach City College
Long Beach 90808
JC-CS-BDP-B
Foothill College
Los Altos Hills 94022
JC-CS-BDP-S-B
California State College
Los Angeles 90032
CS-BDP-S
Los Angeles City College
Los Angeles 90029
JC-CS-BDP-S-B
Loyola University of
Los Angeles
Los Angeles 90045
CS
Mount St. Mary's College
Los Angeles 90049
CS-BDP
Occidental College
Los Angeles 90041
CS-BDP
Pepperdine College
Los Angeles 90044
CS-BDP
University of Southern
California
Los Angeles 90007
CS-BDP
West Coast University
Los Angeles 90005
CS-S
Woodbury College
Los Angeles 90017
BDP
Yuba College
Marysville 95901
JC-CS-BDP

Merced College
Merced 95340
JC-BDP-B
Modesto Jr. College
Modesto 95350
JC-CS-BDP-B
Monterey Peninsula College
Monterey 93940
JC-CS-BDP-B
Napa College
Napa 94558
JC-CS-BDP
San Fernando Valley College
Northridge 91324
CS-BDP
Cerritos College
Norwalk 90650
JC-CS-BDP
Healds Business College
Oakland 94612
JC-CS-BDP
Merritt College
Oakland 94609
JC-CS-BDP-B
Chapman College
Orange 92666
BDP
College of the Desert
Palm Desert 92260
JC-BDP
Pasadena City College
Pasadena 91106
JC-CS-BDP-S-B
Pasadena College
Pasadena 91104
CS-BDP
Shasta College
Redding 96001
JC-BDP
University of Redlands
Redlands 92373
CS-BDP

Reedley College
    Reedley 93654
        JC-CS-BDP
Riverside City College
    Riverside 92506
        JC-CS-BDP-B
University of California
    Riverside 92502
        CS-BDP
Sierra College
    Rocklin 95677
        JC-BDP
American River Jr. College
    Sacramento 95841
        JC-CS-BDP-B
Sacramento State College
    Sacramento 95819
        CS-BDP
Hartnell College
    Salinas 93901
        JC-BDP
San Bernardino Valley College
    San Bernardino 92403
        JC-BDP
San Diego Jr. College
    San Diego 92101
        JC-CS-BDP-B
San Diego Mesa College
    San Diego 92111
        JC-BDP
San Diego State College
    San Diego 92115
        CS-BDP
City College of San Francisco
    San Francisco 94112
        JC-CS-BDP
Golden Gate College
    San Francisco 94012
        BDP
San Francisco State College
    San Francisco 94132
        BDP

San Jose Jr. College
    San Jose 95114
        JC-CS-BDP-B
San Jose State College
    San Jose 95114
        CS-BDP
California State Polytechnic
College
    San Luis Obispo 93401
        CS-BDP
College of San Mateo
    San Mateo 94402
        JC-CS-BDP-S-B
Contra Costa College
    San Pablo 94806
        JC-CS-BDP-B
Santa Ana College
    Santa Ana 92706
        JC-CS-BDP-S-B
Santa Barbara Jr. College
    Santa Barbara 93105
        JC-CS-BDP-B
University of California
    Santa Barbara 93106
        BDP
University of Santa Clara
    Santa Clara 95053
        BDP
Rio Hondo Jr. College
    Santa Fe Springs 90601
        JC-BDP
Allan Hancock College
    Santa Maria 93454
        JC-CS-BDP
Stanford University
    Stanford 94305
        CS-S
University of the Pacific
    Stockton 95204
        CS
Taft College
    Taft 93268
        JC-BDP

California Lutheran College
Thousand Oaks 91360
BDP
Los Angeles Valley College
Van Nuys 91401
JC-CS-BDP-S-B
Ventura College
Ventura 93003
JC-BDP-B
Victor Valley College
Victorville 92392
JC-CS-BDP-B
College of the Sequoias
Visalia 93277
JC-BDP-B
Mount St. Antonio College
Walnut 91789
JC-CS-BDP
Whittier College
Whittier 90608
CS
Los Angeles Pierce Jr. College
Woodland Hills 91364
JC-CS-BDP

COLORADO

Colorado College
Colorado Springs 80903
CS
Regis College
Denver 80221
BDP
University of Denver
Denver 80210
CS-BDP
Colorado State University
Fort Collins 80521
CS-BDP-S-B
Mesa College
Grand Junction 81501
JC-CS-BDP-S-B

Colorado State College
Greeley 80631
CS-BDP
Western State College of
Colorado
Gunnison 81230
BDP
Otero Jr. College
La Junta 81050
JC-BDP-B
Lamar Jr. Community College
Lamar 81052
JC-BDP-S-B
Southern Colorado State College
Pueblo 81005
CS-BDP-S-B
Northeastern Jr. College
Sterling 80751
JC-BDP
Trinidad State Jr. College
Trinidad 81082
JC-CS-BDP-S-B

CONNECTICUT

University of Bridgeport
Bridgeport 06602
BDP
Danbury State College
Danbury 06810
CS-BDP
Quinnipiac College
Hamden 06518
BDP-B
Trinity College
Hartford 06106
CS
Manchester Community College
Manchester 06040
JC-BDP-B
Wesleyan University
Middletown 06457
BDP

Central Connecticut State
  College
    New Britain 06050
      BDP
University of Connecticut
    Storrs 06268
      CS-BDP
Post Jr. College
    Waterbury 06708
      JC-BDP
University of Hartford
    West Hartford 06117
      CS-BDP-B
New Haven College
    West Haven 06516
      CS-BDP-B

DELAWARE

Wesley College
    Dover 19901
      JC-CS-BDP
University of Delaware
    Newark 19711
      CS-BDP-S
Goldey Beacom Jr. College
    Wilmington 19899
      JC-BDP

DISTRICT OF COLUMBIA

The American University
    Washington 20016
      CS-BDP-S-B
Catholic University of America
    Washington 20017
      CS
Dunbarton College of
  Holy Cross
    Washington 20018
      CS-BDP
Strayer Jr. College
    Washington 20005
      JC-BDP-B

FLORIDA
Florida Atlantic University
    Boca Raton 33432
      BDP-B
Marymount College
    Boca Raton 33432
      JC-BDP
Manatee Jr. College
    Bradenton 33505
      JC-CS-BDP-S-B
Brevard Jr. College
    Cocoa 32922
      JC-CS-BDP-S-B
Daytona Beach Jr. College
    Daytona Beach 32015
      JC-BDP
Stetson University
    Deland 32720
      CS
Broward Jr. College
    Ft. Lauderdale 33314
      JC-CS-BDP-B
Edison Jr. College
    Ft. Myers 33901
      JC-BDP
University of Florida
    Gainesville 32601
      CS-BDP
Jones College
    Jacksonville 33211
      BDP-S-B
Palm Beach Jr. College
    Lake Worth 33460
      JC-CS-BDP-S-B
North Florida Jr. College
    Madison 32340
      JC-CS-BDP-S-B
Chipola Jr. College
    Marianna 32446
      JC-CS-BDP
Miami-Dade Jr. College
    Miami 33167
      JC-CS-BDP-S-B

St. John's River Jr. College
Palatka 32077
JC-BDP-B
Gulf Coast Jr. College
Panama City 32401
JC-BDP
Pensacola Jr. College
Pensacola 32504
JC-BDP-B
Florida A & M University
Tallahassee 32306
BDP-B
Florida State University
Tallahassee 32306
CS-BDP
Okaloosa Walton Jr. College
Valparaiso 32580
JC-BDP
Polk Jr. College
Winter Haven 33880
JC-BDP

GEORGIA
Albany State College
Albany 31705
CS-BDP
Georgia Southwestern College
Americus 31709
CS-BDP
University of Georgia
Athens 30601
CS-BDP-S-B
Atlanta University
Atlanta 30314
CS-BDP
Emory University
Atlanta 30322
CS-BDP
Georgia Institute of Technology
Atlanta 30332
BDP
Georgia State College
Atlanta 30303
CS-BDP-B

Brunswick Jr. College
Brunswick 31520
JC-BDP
Middle Georgia College
Cochran 31014
JC-BDP
South Georgia College
Douglas 31533
JC-BDP
Valdosta State College
Valdosta 31601
BDP

HAWAII
Maunaolu College
Paia Maui 96779
JC-CS-BDP

IDAHO
Boise State College
Boise 83701
BDP
University of Idaho
Moscow 83843
CS-BDP
Idaho State University
Pocatello 83201
CS-BDP

ILLINOIS
Aurora College
Aurora 60507
CS-BDP
Illinois Wesleyan University
Bloomington 61701
BDP
Southern Illinois University
Carbondale 62901
CS-BDP-B
Eastern Illinois University
Charleston 61920
CS-BDP

Chicago City College
    Chicago 60634
        JC-BDP
DePaul University
    Chicago 60604
        BDP
Illinois Institute of Technology
    Chicago 60616
        CS-BDP-S
Loyola University
    Chicago 60611
        CS-BDP
Roosevelt University
    Chicago 60605
        CS-BDP
University of Chicago
    Chicago 60637
        CS
Danville Jr. College
    Danville 61832
        JC-CS-BDP-B
Millikin University
    Decatur 62522
        BDP
Northern Illinois University
    DeKalb 60115
        CS-BDP
Elgin Community College
    Elgin 60120
        JC-BDP
Principia College
    Elsah 62028
        CS
Joliet Jr. College
    Joliet 60432
        JC-BDP
Lyons Township Jr. College
    LaGrange 60525
        JC-BDP-B
LaSalle-Peru-Oglesby Jr. College
    La Salle 61301
        JC-BDP

Lewis College
    Lockport 60441
        CS-BDP
Black Hawk College
    Moline 61265
        JC-CS
Wabash Valley College
    Mt. Carmel 62863
        JC-CS-BDP
Illinois State University
    Normal 61761
        CS-BDP
Bradley University
    Peoria 61606
        CS-BDP-S
Rosary College
    River Forest 60305
        CS
Augustana College
    Rock Island 61201
        CS-BDP
University of Illinois
    Urbana 61801
        CS-BDP-S
Wheaton College
    Wheaton 60187
        CS-BDP

INDIANA

Anderson College
    Anderson 46011
        CS-BDP
Tri-State College
    Angola 46703
        CS-BDP
Evansville College
    Evansville 47704
        CS-BDP
DePauw University
    Greencastle 46135
        CS-BDP-S

Butler University
    Indianapolis 46208
        BDP
Marian College
    Indianapolis 46222
        CS
Purdue University
    Lafayette 47907
        CS-BDP-S
Ball State College
    Muncie 47306
        CS-BDP
University of Notre Dame
    Notre Dame 46556
        CS-BDP
St. Joseph's College
    Rensselaer 47978
        CS-BDP
Indiana State College
    Terre Haute 47809
        CS-BDP
Valparaiso University
    Valparaiso 46383
        CS-BDP

IOWA

Iowa State University of Science
    & Technology
    Ames 50010
        CS-BDP-S
Iowa State College
    Cedar Falls 50613
        CS-BDP
Coe College
    Cedar Rapids 52402
        CS
St. Ambrose College
    Davenport 52803
        S
Luther College
    Decorah 52101
        CS-BDP

Drake University
    Des Moines 50311
        CS-BDP
Clarke College
    Dubuque 52001
        CS-BDP
Loras College
    Dubuque 52001
        CS
Parsons College
    Fairfield 52556
        BDP
Iowa Central Community
    College
    Fort Dodge 50501
        JC-BDP
University of Iowa
    Iowa City 52240
        CS-BDP-S

KANSAS

Butler County Community Jr.
    College
    El Dorado 67042
        JC-BDP-B
Fort Hays Kansas State College
    Hays 67601
        CS-BDP
Kansas City Kansas Community
    Jr. College
    Kansas City 66101
        JC-BDP
University of Kansas
    Lawrence 66044
        CS-BDP
Central College
    McPherson 67460
        JC-BDP
Kansas State University of
    Agriculture & Applied Science
    Manhattan 66502
        BDP-B

Kansas State College of
  Pittsburg
    Pittsburg 66762
      BDP-B
Pratt Community Jr. College
    Pratt 67124
      JC-BDP
Kansas Wesleyan University
    Salina 67401
      CS
Washburn University of Topeka
    Topeka 66621
      CS-BDP
Friends University
    Wichita 67213
      BDP
Sacred Heart College
    Wichita 67213
      CS-BDP
Wichita State University
    Wichita 67208
      CS-BDP

KENTUCKY

Union College
    Barbourville 40906
      BDP
Western Kentucky University
    Bowling Green 42101
      BDP
Bellarmine-Ursuline College
    Louisville 40205
      BDP-B
University of Louisville
    Louisville 40208
      CS-BDP
Murray State University
    Murray 42071
      CS-BDP
Brescia College
    Owensboro 42301
      BDP

Paducah Community College
    Paducah 42001
      JC-BDP
Eastern Kentucky University
    Richmond 40475
      BDP-B
Asbury College
    Wilmore 40390
      CS

LOUISIANA

Louisiana State University
    Baton Rouge 70803
      BDP
Grambling College
    Grambling 71245
      CS-BDP
Southeastern Louisiana College
    Hammond 70401
      CS-BDP
University of Southwestern
  Louisiana
    Lafayette 70501
      CS-BDP-S-B
McNeese State College
    Lake Charles 70601
      CS
Northeast Louisiana State
  College
    Monroe 71201
      CS-BDP
Loyola University
    New Orleans 70118
      CS-BDP-S
Tulane University
    New Orleans 70118
      CS-BDP
Louisiana Polytechnic Institute
    Ruston 71270
      CS-BDP-B
Francis T. Nicholls State College
    Thibodaux 70301
      CS-BDP

MAINE
Husson College
Bangor 04401
BDP
Bowdoin College
Brunswick 04011
CS
University of Maine
Orono 04473
CS-BDP
Colby College
Waterville 04901
CS-BDP

MARYLAND

Baltimore College of Commerce
Baltimore 21201
BDP
Community College of
Baltimore
Baltimore 21215
JC-BDP-B
Johns Hopkins University
Baltimore 21218
CS
Loyola College
Baltimore 21210
CS-BDP
Mount St. Agnes College
Baltimore 21209
CS
University of Baltimore
Baltimore 21201
BDP
Harford Jr. College
Bel Air 21014
JC-CS-BDP-B
Catonsville Community College
Catonsville 21228
JC-BDP-B
University of Maryland
College Park 20740
CS-BDP

Hagerstown Jr. College
Hagerstown 21740
JC-BDP
Charles County Community
College
La Plata 20646
JC-CS-BDP
Prince Georges Community
College
Suitland 20870
JC-CS-BDP
Montgomery Jr. College
Takoma Park 20012
JC-CS-S
Goucher College
Towson 21204
CS
Western Maryland College
Westminster 21157
CS

MASSACHUSETTS

Chamberlayne Jr. College
Boston 02116
JC-CS-BDP-S-B
Northeastern University
Boston 02115
CS-BDP-B
Simmons College
Boston 02115
CS
Harvard University
Cambridge 02138
CS-BDP-S-B
Massachusetts Institute of
Technology
Cambridge 02139
CS-BDP-S-B
Nichols College of Business
Administration
Dudley 01570
BDP

State College at Fitchburg
  Fitchburg 01420
    CS
State College at Framingham
  Framingham 01701
    BDP
Mount Wachusett Community
  College
    Gardner 01440
      JC-BDP
Northern Essex Community
  College
    Haverhill 01830
      JC-CS-BDP-S
Holyoke Community College
  Holyoke 01040
    JC-BDP-B
Atlantic Union College
  Lancaster 01561
    CS-BDP
Lowell Technological Institute
  Lowell 01854
    CS-BDP
Newton Jr. College
  Newtonville 02160
    JC-CS-BDP-S-B
State College at North Adams
  North Adams 01247
    BDP
Northampton Commercial
  College
    Northampton 01060
      JC-BDP
Smith College
  Northampton 01060
    CS
Berkshire Community College
  Pittsfield 01201
    JC-BDP
Brandeis University
  Waltham 02154
    CS

Clark University
  Worcester 01610
    CS-BDP
College of the Holy Cross
  Worcester 01610
    CS
Worcester Jr. College
  Worcester 01608
    JC-CS-BDP

MICHIGAN
Kellogg Community College
  Battle Creek 49016
    JC-CS-BDP-S-B
Ferris State College
  Big Rapids 49307
    BDP-B
Detroit College of Business
  Dearborn 48126
    BDP-B
Detroit Institute of Technology
  Detroit 48201
    BDP-B
University of Detroit
  Detroit 48221
    CS-BDP
Grand Rapids Jr. College
  Grand Rapids 49502
    JC-CS-BDP-S-B
Hope College
  Holland 49423
    CS
Jackson Community College
  Jackson 49201
    JC-BDP
Kalamazoo College
  Kalamazoo 49001
    CS
Western Michigan University
  Kalamazoo 49001
    CS-BDP-B
Lansing Community College
  Lansing 48914
    JC-CS-BDP-B

Schoolcraft College
Livonia 48151
JC-BDP-B
Northern Michigan University
Marquette 49855
CS-S
Northwood Institute
Midland 48640
JC-BDP
Central Michigan University
Mt. Pleasant 48858
CS-BDP
Nazareth College
Nazareth 49074
CS
Lawrence Institute of
Technology
Southfield 48075
CS-BDP
Delta College
University Center 48710
JC-BDP-B
Macomb County Community
College
Warren 48093
JC-BDP-B
Cleary College
Ypsilanti 48197
BDP

MINNESOTA
Bemidji State College
Bemidji 56601
BDP
St. John University
Collegeville 56321
CS-BDP
Mankato State College
Mankato 56001
BDP
University of Minnesota
Minneapolis 55455
CS-BDP-S-B

Concordia College
Moorhead 56560
CS
Moorhead State College
Moorhead 56560
CS-BDP
St. Cloud State College
St. Cloud 56301
BDP
College of St. Thomas
St. Paul 55101
CS-BDP
Gustavus Adolphus College
St. Peter 56082
BDP
College of St. Theresa
Winona 55987
CS-BDP
Winona State College
Winona 55987
CS-BDP
Worthington State Jr. College
Worthington 56187
JC-BDP-B

MISSISSIPPI
Northeast Mississippi
Jr. College
Booneville 38829
JC-BDP
Mississippi State College
for Women
Columbus 39701
BDP
Jones County Jr. College
Ellisville 39437
BDP
University of Southern
Mississippi
Hattiesburg 39401
CS-S
Hinds Jr. College
Raymond 39154
JC-CS-BDP-B

Mississippi State University
State College 39762
CS-BDP-B
University of Mississippi
University 38677
BDP
Capiah Lincoln Jr. College
Wesson 39191
BDP-B

MISSOURI

Lincoln University
Jefferson City 65101
CS-BDP
Central Technical Institute
Kansas City 64108
BDP
Metropolitan Jr. College
Kansas City 64111
JC-CS-BDP-B
Rockhurst College
Kansas City 64110
CS
University of Missouri
Kansas City 64110
CS-BDP
Northeast Missouri State
College
Kirksville 63501
CS-BDP
Northwest Missouri State
College
Maryville 64468
BDP
University of Missouri
Rolla 65401
CS-BDP-S
Drury College
Springfield 65802
BDP
Evangel
Springfield 65802
BDP

Southwest Missouri State
College
Springfield 65802
CS-BDP
Lindenwood College
St. Charles 63301
CS-BDP
Maryville College
St. Louis 63141
CS
St. Louis University
St. Louis 63103
CS-BDP
University of Missouri
St. Louis 63121
CS-BDP
Central Missouri State College
Warrensburg 64093
CS-BDP

MONTANA

Montana State University
Bozeman 59715
CS-BDP
College of Great Falls
Great Falls 59401
BDP
Custer County Jr. College
Miles City 59301
JC-CS-BDP
University of Montana
Missoula 59801
CS-BDP

NEBRASKA

Kearney State College
Kearney 68847
CS-BDP
Union College
Lincoln 68506
CS-BDP
McCook College
McCook 69001
JC-CS-BDP

Creighton University
    Omaha 68131
        CS-BDP
Municipal University of Omaha
    Omaha 68101
        CS

NEW HAMPSHIRE

New Hampshire Technical
    Institute
        Concord 03301
            JC-BDP-B
University of New Hampshire
    Durham 03824
        BDP
Dartmouth College
    Hanover 03755
        CS-BDP
New Hampshire College of
    Acctg. & Commerce
        Manchester 03101
            CS-BDP-S-B

NEW JERSEY

Caldwell College for Women
    Caldwell 07006
        CS
Upsala College
    East Orange 07017
        CS-BDP
Jersey City Jr. College
    Jersey City 07306
        JC-CS
St. Peter's College
    Jersey City 07306
        CS-BDP
Drew University
    Madison 07940
        CS
Rutgers University
    New Brunswick 08902
        CS

Princeton University
    Princeton 08540
        CS
Fairleigh Dickinson University
    Rutherford 07070
        CS-BDP-B
Seton Hall University
    South Orange 07079
        CS-BDP
Fairleigh Dickinson University
    Teaneck 07666
        CS-BDP
Rider College
    Trenton 08602
        BDP
Trenton Jr. College
    Trenton 08608
        JC-CS-BDP-S

NEW MEXICO

University of New Mexico
    Albuquerque 87106
        CS-BDP
New Mexico Highlands
    University
        Las Vegas 87701
            CS-BDP
Eastern New Mexico University
    Portales 88130
        CS-BDP-B
New Mexico State University
    University Park 88070
        JC-CS-BDP-B

NEW YORK

State University of New York
    Albany 12201
        CS-BDP
Alfred University
    Alfred 14802
        CS-BDP-S-B
Auburn Community College
    Auburn 13021
        JC-CS-BDP-B

Wells College
  Aurora 13026
    CS
Queensborough Community
  College
    Bayside 11364
      JC-BDP
Broome Technical Community
  College
    Binghamton 13902
      JC-CS-BDP
Bronx Community College
  Bronx 10468
    JC
Fordham University
  Bronx 10458
    CS-BDP
Kingsborough Community
  College
    Brooklyn 11235
      JC-CS-BDP-S-B
New York City Community
  College
    Brooklyn 11201
      JC-BDP-B
Polytechnic Institute of Brooklyn
  Brooklyn 11201
    CS
Pratt Institute
  Brooklyn 11205
    CS-S
Canisius College
  Buffalo 14208
    CS-BDP
Erie County Technical Institute
  Buffalo 14221
    JC-CS-BDP-S-B
State University of New York
  Buffalo 14214
    CS
State University of New York
  Canton 13617
    JC-BDP-B

Hamilton College
  Clinton 13323
    CS
Corning Community College
  Corning 14830
    JC-BDP-B
State University of New York
  Delhi 13753
    JC-BDP
Elmira College
  Elmira 14901
    BDP
State University of New York
  Farmingdale 11735
    JC-BDP
Queens College
  Flushing 11367
    CS
Adelphi University
  Garden City 11530
    CS-BDP-B
Nassau Community College
  Garden City 11530
    JC-CS-BDP
Adirondack Community College
  Glen Falls 12801
    JC-BDP
Colgate University
  Hamilton 13346
    CS
Hofstra University
  Hempstead 11550
    CS-BDP-S
Cornell University
  Ithaca 14950
    CS-BDP-S
Ithaca College
  Ithaca 14950
    CS-BDP
Jamestown Community College
  Jamestown 14701
    JC-BDP

St. Bernardine of Sienna College
Loudonville 12211
CS-BDP

Orange County Community
College
Middletown 10940
JC-BDP

State University of New York
Morrisville 13408
JC-BDP-B

State University of New York
New Paltz 12561
CS

Iona College
New Rochelle 10804
BDP

Borough of Manhattan
Community College
New York 10020
JC

City College of New York
New York 10010
BDP-B

Columbia University
New York 10027
BDP

Cooper Union
New York 10003
CS

New York University
New York 10003
CS-BDP

Pace College
New York 10038
BDP-B

Niagara County Community
College
Niagara Falls 14303
JC-BDP

State University of New York
Oswego 13126
CS

State University of New York
Plattsburgh 12901
CS

Dutchess Community College
Poughkeepsie 12601
JC-BDP-B

Vassar College
Poughkeepsie 12601
CS

Clarkson College of Technology
Potsdam 13676
CS-BDP

State University of New York
Potsdam 13676
CS-BDP

Monroe Community College
Rochester 14607
BDP-B

Union University
Schenectady 12308
CS

Suffolk County Community
College
Selden 11784
JC-CS-BDP-B

Staten Island Community
College
Staten Island 10301
JC-BDP

Wagner College
Staten Island 10301
BDP

Ulster County Community
College
Stone Ridge 12484
JC-BDP

State University of New York
Stony Brook 11790
CS

Onondaga Community College
Syracuse 13210
JC-CS

Syracuse University
  Syracuse 13210
    CS-BDP-S
Hudson Valley Community
  College
    Troy 12180
      JC-CS-BDP-B
Rensselaer Polytechnic Institute
  Troy 12180
    CS-BDP
Westchester Community College
  Valhalla 10595
    JC-CS
Jefferson Community College
  Watertown 13601
    JC-BDP
Elizabeth Seton College
  Yonkers 10701
    BDP

NORTH CAROLINA
  Gardner Webb College
    Boiling Springs 28017
      JC-BDP
  Appalachian State Teachers
    College
      Boone 28608
        CS
  University of North Carolina
    Chapel Hill 27514
      CS-BDP-S-B
  Johnson C. Smith University
    Charlotte 28208
      CS
  Kings College
    Charlotte 28201
      JC-BDP
  Barber-Scotia College
    Concord 28025
      BDP
  Western Carolina University
    Cullowhee 28723
      CS-BDP

Davidson College
  Davidson 28036
    CS
Duke University
  Durham 27706
    CS-BDP
North Carolina College
  Durham 27707
    CS-BDP
College of the Albemarle
  Elizabeth City 27909
    JC-CS-S-B
Elizabeth City State College
  Elizabeth City 27909
    BDP
Elon College
  Elon 27244
    BDP
Bennett College
  Greensboro 27420
    CS
East Carolina College
  Greenville 27834
    CS-BDP
Guilford College
  Guilford 27410
    CS
High Point College
  High Point 27262
    BDP
Wilmington College
  Wilmington 28401
    CS-BDP
Wake Forest University
  Winston Salem 27109
    CS

NORTH DAKOTA

  North Dakota State University
    Fargo 58102
      CS

University of North Dakota
Grand Forks 58201
CS-BDP
North Dakota State School
of Science
Wahpeton 58075
JC-BDP-S-B

OHIO

Ohio Northern University
Ada 45810
BDP
Ohio University
Athens 45701
CS-BDP
University of Akron
Akron 44304
CS-BDP
Bowling Green State University
Bryan 43506
CS-BDP
Walsh College
Canton 44720
BDP
University of Cincinnati
Cincinnati 45221
CS-BDP
Ohio College of Applied Science
Cincinnati 45210
JC-CS-BDP
Case Western Reserve University
Cleveland 44106
CS-BDP
Cuyahoga Community College
Cleveland 44115
JC-BDP-B
John Carroll University
Cleveland 44118
CS-BDP
Notre Dame College
Cleveland 44121
CS-BDP

Bliss College
Columbus 43215
BDP
Franklin University
Columbus 43215
BDP
Ohio State University
Columbus 43210
CS-BDP-S
Sinclair Community College
Dayton 45402
JC-CS-BDP-B
University of Dayton
Dayton 45409
CS-BDP-S
Defiance College
Defiance 43512
CS
Ohio Wesleyan University
Delaware 43015
CS
Kent State University
Kent 44240
CS-BDP
Marietta College
Marietta 45750
BDP
Muskingum College
New Concord 43762
CS
Oberlin College
Oberlin 44074
CS
Miami University
Oxford 45056
CS-BDP-S
Wittenberg University
Springfield 45501
BDP
College of Steubenville
Steubenville 43952
BDP

University of Toledo
Toledo 43606
BDP-B
Central State College
Wilberforce 45384
BDP
College of Wooster
Wooster 44691
CS-BDP
Penn Ohio Jr. College
Youngstown 44507
JC-CS-BDP
Youngstown State University
Youngstown 44503
CS-BDP

OKLAHOMA

East Central State College
Ada 74820
CS-BDP
Altus Jr. College
Altus 73521
JC-BDP-S-B
Bethany Nazarene College
Bethany 73008
BDP
Oklahoma College of
Liberal Arts
Chickasha 73018
CS-BDP
Central State College
Edmond 73034
BDP-B
Cameron State Agricultural
College
Lawton 73051
CS-BDP-B
Northeastern Oklahoma A & M
College
Miami 74354
JC-BDP-B
University of Oklahoma
Norman 73069
CS-BDP-S-B

Oklahoma Christian College
Oklahoma City 73111
CS-BDP
Oklahoma City University
Oklahoma City 73106
BDP
Oklahoma State University
Stillwater 74074
CS-BDP
Northeastern State College
Tahlequah 74464
CS-BDP
Northern Oklahoma Jr. College
Tonkawa 74653
JC-CS-BDP-B
University of Tulsa
Tulsa 74104
CS-BDP
Southwestern State College
Weatherford 73096
CS-S
Eastern Oklahoma State College
Wilburton 74578
JC-CS-BDP-B

OREGON

Southern Oregon College
Ashland 97520
CS-BDP
Clatsop Community College
Astoria 97103
JC-BDP
Oregon State University
Corvallis 97331
CS-BDP
University of Oregon
Eugene 97403
CS-BDP-B
Pacific University
Forest Grove 97116
CS-BDP
Oregon Technical Institute
Klamath Falls 97601
CS-BDP-S

Eastern Oregon College
La Grande 97850
BDP
Linfield College
McMinnville 97129
CS
Portland Community College
Portland 97201
JC-BDP-B
Portland State College
Portland 97207
CS
University of Portland
Portland 97203
CS-BDP
Willamette University
Salem 97301
CS

PENNSYLVANIA
Muhlenberg College
Allentown 18104
CS
Penn State University
Allentown 18102
JC-BDP
Penn State University
Altoona 16001
JC-CS
Geneva College
Beaver Falls 15010
CS-BDP
Lehigh University
Bethlehem 18105
CS-BDP
Bloomsburg State College
Bloomsburg 17815
BDP
Clarion State College
Clarion 16214
CS-BDP
East Stroudsberg College
East Stroudsberg 18301
CS-BDP

Edinboro State College
Edinboro 16412
CS
Elizabethtown College
Elizabethtown 17022
BDP
Penn State University
Erie 16510
JC-CS-BDP
Seton Hall College
Greensburg 15601
CS
Harrisburg Area Community
College
Harrisburg 17110
JC-CS-BDP-S-B
Juniata College
Huntingdon 16652
CS
Indiana University of
Pennsylvania
Indiana 15701
CS-BDP
St. Vincent College
Latrobe 15650
CS
Bucknell University
Lewisburg 17837
CS-BDP-S
Lock Haven State College
Lock Haven 17745
CS
St. Francis College
Loretto 15940
CS
Mansfield State College
Mansfield 16933
CS
Allegheny College
Meadville 16335
CS
Millersville State College
Millersville 17551
CS

Drexel Institute of Technology
Philadelphia 19104
CS-BDP-B
Peirce Jr. College
Philadelphia 19102
JC-BDP-S-B
St. Josephs College
Philadelphia 19131
BDP
Temple University
Philadelphia 19122
CS-BDP-B
Carnegie-Mellon University
Pittsburgh 15213
CS-S
Point Park Jr. College
Pittsburgh 15222
BDP-B
Robert Morris Jr. College
Pittsburgh 15219
JC-BDP
University of Pittsburgh
Pittsburgh 15213
CS-BDP-S

Marywood College
Scranton 18509
CS-BDP
University of Scranton
Scranton 18510
CS-BDP
Shippensburg State College
Shippensburg 17257
CS-BDP
Pennsylvania State University
University Park 16802
CS-BDP-S
Waynesburg College
Waynesburg 15370
BDP
West Chester State College
West Chester 19380
CS

Kings College
Wilkes Barre 18702
BDP-B
Penn State University
Wilkes Barre 18705
JC-CS
Lycoming College
Williamsport 17701
BDP
Williamsport Community
College
Williamsport 17701
JC-CS-BDP-S-B
York Jr. College
York 17405
JC-CS-BDP

PUERTO RICO
Catholic University of
Puerto Rico
Ponce 00731
CS-BDP-B
University of Puerto Rico
Rio Piedras 00931
BDP

RHODE ISLAND
Johnson & Walker Jr. College
Providence 02903
JC-BDP-B
Providence College
Providence 02918
CS-BDP
Rhode Island College
Providence 02908
CS

SOUTH CAROLINA
Citadel
Charleston 29409
CS-BDP
Palmer College
Charleston 19401
JC-BDP-B

Clemson University
Clemson 19631
CS-S
Bob Jones Academy
Greenville 29614
JC-CS
Winthrop College
Rock Hill 29730
CS-BDP-S

SOUTH DAKOTA
Northern State College
Aberdeen 57401
BDP
South Dakota School of Mines
& Technology
Rapid City 57701
CS
Sioux Falls College
Sioux Falls 57101
CS-BDP
Black Hills State College
Spearfish 57783
BDP
Southern State College
Springfield 57062
BDP

TENNESSEE
Lee College
Cleveland 37311
BDP
East Tennessee State University
Johnson City 37601
CS-BDP
Steed College
Johnson City 37603
BDP-B
University of Tennessee
Knoxville 37920
CS-BDP-S-B
University of Tennessee
Martin 38237
BDP

Christian Brothers College
Memphis 38104
CS-BDP
Memphis State University
Memphis 38111
CS-BDP
Middle Tennessee State College
Murfreesboro 37130
CS-BDP
Vanderbilt University
Nashville 37203
CS
University of the South
Sewanee 37375
CS

TEXAS
Abilene Christian College
Abilene 79601
BDP
Hardin Simmons University
Abilene 79601
BDP
McMurry College
Abilene 79605
CS
Alvin Jr. College
Alvin 77511
JC-BDP-B
Amarillo College
Amarillo 79105
JC-BDP-B
University of Texas
Arlington 76010
CS-BDP-B
Henderson County Jr. College
Athens 75751
JC-BDP-S-B
St. Edwards University
Austin 78704
CS-BDP
University of Texas
Austin 78712
CS-BDP

Lee College
Baytown 77520
JC-CS-BDP-B

Frank Phillips College
Borger 79007
JC-BDP

Texas Southmost College
Brownsville 78520
JC-BDP

Howard Payne College
Brownwood 76801
BDP

West Texas State University
Canyon 79015
BDP-B

Texas A & M University
College Station 77843
CS-BDP-S-B

Del Mar College
Corpus Christi 78404
JC-BDP

Navarro Jr. College
Corsicana 75110
JC-BDP-B

Southern Methodist University
Dallas 75222
BDP-B

Grayson County Jr. College
Denison 75020
JC-BDP-B

Pan American College
Edinburg 78539
BDP

Texas Christian University
Fort Worth 76129
BDP

Cooke County Jr. College
Gainsville 76240
JC-CS-BDP

Southwestern University
Georgetown 78626
CS-BDP

Hill Jr. College
Hillsboro 76645
JC-CS-BDP

Houston Baptist College
Houston 77036
BDP

University of Houston
Houston 77004
CS-BDP-S

Kilgore College
Kilgore 75662
JC-BDP-B

Laredo Jr. College
Laredo 78040
JC-BDP

South Plains College
Levelland 79336
JC-CS-BDP-B

LeTourneau College
Longview 75601
CS-BDP

Texas University
Lubbock 79409
BDP

Stephen F. Austin State College
Nacogdoches 75962
CS-BDP

Paris Jr. College
Paris 75460
JC-BDP

San Jacinto College
Pasadena 77505
JC-BDP-B

San Angelo College
San Angelo 76901
CS-BDP

St. Marys University
San Antonio 78228
CS-BDP

Tarleton State College
Stephenville 76401
CS-BDP

Temple Jr. College
  Temple 76501
    JC-BDP
Texarkana College
  Texarkana 75501
    JC-CS-BDP
Tyler Jr. College
  Tyler 75701
    JC-BDP-S-B
Southwest Texas Jr. College
  Uvalde 78801
    JC-BDP
Baylor University
  Waco 76703
    BDP
Weatherford Jr. College
  Weatherford 76086
    JC-CS-BDP-B
Wharton County Jr. College
  Wharton 77488
    JC-CS-BDP

UTAH

Utah State University
  Logan 84321
    CS-BDP-S
Weber State College
  Ogden 84403
    CS-B
Brigham Young University
  Provo 84601
    BDP
Latter Day Saints Business
College
  Salt Lake City 84111
    JC-CS-BDP-S-B
University of Utah
  Salt Lake City 84112
    CS-BDP-S
Westminster College
  Salt Lake City 84105
    CS-BDP

VERMONT

University of Vermont
  Burlington 05401
    BDP
Norwich University
  Northfield 05663
    CS-BDP
Windham College
  Putney 05346
    CS-BDP-B

VIRGINIA

Virginia Polytechnic Institute
  Blacksburg 24061
    CS-BDP
Bridgewater College
  Bridgewater 22812
    CS
University of Virginia
  Charlottesville 22903
    CS-S
Danville Community College
  Danville 24541
    JC-CS-BDP
Longwood College
  Farmville 23901
    CS
Hampden Sydney College
  Hampden Sydney 23943
    BDP
Madison College
  Harrisonburg 22802
    CS
Washington & Lee University
  Lexington 24450
    CS
Lynchburg College
  Lynchburg 24504
    BDP
Virginia State College
  Petersburg 23803
    BDP

Richmond Professional Institute
Richmond 23220
JC-CS-BDP-B
University of Richmond
Richmond 23173
CS-BDP
Roanoke College
Salem 24153
CS-BDP
Sweet Briar College
Sweet Briar 24595
CS
College of William & Mary
Williamsburg 23185
BDP
Wytheville Community College
Wytheville 24382
JC-BDP

WASHINGTON

Grays Harbor College
Aberdeen 98520
JC-CS-BDP-B
Green River CommunityCollege
Auburn 98002
JC-BDP
Western Washington State
College
Bellingham 98225
CS
Centralia College
Centralia 98531
JC-BDP-B
Walla Walla College
College Place 99324
BDP
Everett Community College
Everett 98201
JC-CS-BDP-B
Lower Columbia College
Longview 68632
JC-CS-BDP-B

Highline Community College
Midway 98031
JC-BDP-B
Skagit Valley College
Mt. Vernon 98273
JC-BDP
Seattle Pacific College
Seattle 98119
BDP
Seattle University
Seattle 98112
CS-BDP
University of Washington
Seattle 98105
BDP-S
Gonzaga University
Spokane 99202
CS-BDP
Spokane Community College
Spokane 99204
JC-CS-BDP
Whitworth College
Spokane 99218
CS-BDP
Pacific Lutheran University
Tacoma 98447
BDP
University of Puget Sound
Tacoma 98416
CS-BDP
Clark College
Vancouver 98663
JC-BDP-B
Whitman College
Walla Walla 99362
CS-BDP
Yakima Valley College
Yakima 98902
JC-BDP
WEST VIRGINIA
Concord College
Athens 24712
BDP

Fairmont State College
  Fairmont 26554
    BDP
Potomac State College of
  West Virginia
    Keyser 26726
      JC-CS-BDP
West Virginia Institute of
  Technology
    Montgomery 25136
      CS-BDP
West Virginia University
  Morgantown 26506
    CS
West Liberty State College
  West Liberty 26074
    BDP

WISCONSIN

Lawrence University
  Appleton 54911
    CS
Beloit College
  Beloit 53511
    CS-BDP-S
Wisconsin State University
  Eau Claire 54701
    CS-BDP
University of Wisconsin
  Green Bay 54305
    JC-CS
Carthage College
  Kenosha 53140
    BDP
Wisconsin State University
  La Crosse 54601
    CS
University of Wisconsin
  Madison 53706
    CS-BDP-S-B

Stout State University
  Menomonie 54751
    CS
Marquette University
  Milwaukee 53233
    BDP
Milwaukee Institute of
  Technology
    Milwaukee 53203
      CS-BDP-S-B
University of Wisconsin
  Milwaukee 53201
    CS-BDP-B
Wisconsin State University
  Oshkosh 54901
    CS-BDP
Wisconsin State University
  Platteville 53818
    CS
Wisconsin State University
  River Falls 54022
    CS-BDP-S-B
Carroll College
  Waukesha 53186
    CS
St. Norbert College
  West De Pere 54178
    BDP
Wisconsin State University
  Whitewater 53190
    CS-BDP-B

WYOMING

Casper College
  Casper 82601
    JC-BDP-B
University of Wyoming
  Laramie 82070
    CS-BDP
Northwest Community College
  Powell 82435
    JC-CS-BDP

APPENDIX C

CORRESPONDENCE OR HOME STUDY SCHOOLS

WHILE EVERY ATTEMPT was made to make this listing as complete as possible, some reputable schools may be missing. This is unintentional. Exclusion does not imply disapproval in any way. On the other hand, inclusion of a school in this listing does not imply approval of the school, its curricula, or its business practices.

Before selecting any particular school, read Chapter 4, "Education and Training," thoroughly. That chapter outlines specific procedures for checking a school's credentials.

LEGEND: * Indicates accreditation by Accrediting Commission of the National Home Study Council.

* American Automation Training Centers, Inc., 2022 Main St., Kansas City, Mo. 64108. Courses in data processing, including tabulating, computer operation, and programing. Terminal resident training required.
* American Computer Institute, 300 Park Ave. S., New York, N.Y. 10010. A programed instruction course in IBM computer programing, including RPG and COBOL languages. A tape recorded course in computer management.

* Automation Training, Inc., 5701 Waterman Ave., St. Louis, Mo. 63112. Courses in tabulation, wiring, and programing on IBM 1401 and 360 equipment. A division of Technical Education Corp.
* Bell & Howell Schools, 4141 W. Belmont Ave., Chicago, Ill. 60641. Courses in computer control electronics, electronics automation technology, and basic programing using IBM 360 equipment.
* Business Electronics, 209 W. Jackson Blvd., Chicago, Ill. 60606. Courses in programing and systems design for business applications, and business data processing for accountants. A division of International Accountants Society, Inc.

University of California, Dept. of Correspondence Instruction, Berkeley, Calif. 94720. Computers and data processing, and programing in FORTRAN.

* Commercial Trades Institute, 1400 W. Greenleaf Ave., Chicago, Ill. 60626. Courses in basic programing, number systems, and software with an option of one of four languages—RPG, BAL, COBOL, or FORTRAN.

Computer Research Institute, 9506 W. Magnolia Ave., P.O. Box 7355, Riverside, Calif. 92503. Fundamentals of computers, System 360 assembler language, FORTRAN IV, and COBOL.

Computer Usage Education, 51 Madison Ave., New York, N.Y. 10010. Computer programing.

* CREI Home Study Div., McGraw-Hill Book Co., 3224 Sixteenth St., N.W., Washington, D.C. 20010. College-level programs in computers.

Data Processing Management Association, 505 Busse Hwy., Park Ridge, Ill. 60068. Understanding automation and computers.

* DeVry Institute of Technology, 4141 W. Belmont Ave., Chicago, Ill. 60641. Courses in computer control electronics, electronic automation technology, and basic computer programing using IBM 360 equipment. A division of Bell & Howell Schools.
* Grantham School of Engineering, 1505 N. Western Ave., Hollywood, Calif. 90027. Courses leading to associate degrees in engineering mathematics and computers.

Ft. Lauderdale Technical College, 201 W. Sunrise Blvd., Ft. Lauderdale, Fla. 33311. Programing for the IBM 360.

Institute For Computing Sciences, 241 Garden Mall, Exchange Pk., Dallas, Tex. 75235. Fundamentals of edp, systems analysis and design, and programing IBM 360 assembly language.

* Institute of Business and Computer Education, 4141 W. Belmont Ave., Chicago, Ill. 60641. Courses in programing using IBM 360 equipment. A division of Bell & Howell Schools.

International Accountants Society, 209 W. Jackson Blvd., Chicago, Ill. 60606. Programing for business computers and business data processing.

* International Correspondence Schools, Scranton, Pa. 18515. Courses in programing and computer technology.

International Data Processing Institute, 7023 E. Kirby St., Detroit, Mich. 48211. Data processing systems and procedures.

* LaSalle Extension University, 417 S. Dearborn St., Chicago, Ill. 60605. Courses in programing.

Lincoln Extension Institute, 1401 W. 75th St., Cleveland, Ohio 44102. Introduction to data processing, understanding the use of computers, and systems analysis and design.

Commonwealth of Massachusetts, Dept. of Education, Bureau of Extended Services, 182 Tremont St., Boston, Mass. 02111. Basic programing.

University of Minnesota, General Extension Div., Dept. of Independent Study, 250 Nicholson Hall, Minneapolis, Minn. 55455. Introduction to digital computers and programing.

University of Missouri, Correspondence Study Dept., 214 Waters Hall, Columbia, Mo. 65201. Introduction to programing and computing.

* North American Institute of Systems and Procedures, 4401 Birch St., Newport Beach, Calif. 92660. Systems and procedures.

Oregon State System of Higher Education, Office of Independent Study, 1724 Moss St., Eugene, Ore. 97403. Introductory edp, and computer programing in FORTRAN.

Pennsylvania State University, Correspondence Study Dept., 3 Shields Bldg., University Pk., Pa. 16802. Punched card data processing principles, punched card data processing applications, principles of programing, and basic computer electronics with applications.

Philco Technical Institute, 219 N. Broad St., Phila., Pa. 19107. Digital computer fundamentals, and programing for digital computers.

* RCA Institutes, Inc., 320 W. 31st St., New York, N.Y. 10001. Courses in digital electronics, automation electronics, and programing.

Technical Education Corp., 5701 Waterman Ave., St. Louis, Mo. 63112. Courses in tabulation, programing on IBM 1401 and 360 equipment, and COBOL.

University of Utah, Correspondence Study Dept., 1213 Annex, P.O. Box 200, Salt Lake City, Utah 84110. Basic computer science concepts, elementary programing, and FORTRAN programing.

Xerox Corporation, Education Div., 600 Madison Ave., New York, N.Y. 10022. Binary arithmetic, and introduction to edp.

SUGGESTED READING

THE FOLLOWING IS A LIST of suggested reading to broaden your base of knowledge of edp. The list is by no means complete, nor was it meant to be. These books will provide you with a good background, and will enable you to discover other sources of information.

Two additional sources of books are your school and local public libraries. Librarians in both will be able to help you find other books of interest.

Allen, Paul, *Exploring the Computer*. Reading, Mass.: Addison-Wesley Publ. Co., 1967.

Barnett, Leo and Lou Ellen Davis, *Careers in Computer Programing*. New York, N.Y.: Henry Z. Walck, Inc., 1967.

Benrey, Ronald M., *Understanding Digital Computers*. New York, N.Y.: John F. Rider, 1964.

Bauer, Charles R., Anthony P. Peluso and William S. Worley, *Iitran 360, Self Instructional Manual and Text*. Reading, Mass.: Addison-Wesley Publ. Co., 1967.

Claffey, William J., *Principles of Data Processing*. Belmont, Calif.: Dickenson Publ. Co., 1967.

Coan, James C., *Basic BASIC: An Introduction to Computer Programing in BASIC Language*. New York, N.Y.: Hayden Book Co., 1970.

Colbert, Douglas A., *Data Processing Concepts*. New York, N.Y.: Mc-Graw-Hill Book Co., 1968.

Crawford, F. R., *Introduction to Data Processing*. Englewood Cliffs, N.J.: Prentice-Hall, 1968.

Davis, Gordon B., *An Introduction to Electronic Computers*. New York, N.Y.: McGraw-Hill Book Co., 1966.

Davis, Sidney, *Your Future in Computer Programing*. New York, N.Y.: Richard Rosen Press, Inc., 1969.

Digital Equipment Corp., *Introduction to Programing*. Maynard, Mass.: Digital Equipment Corp., 1969.

Farina, Mario V., *Computers, A Self Teaching Introduction*. Englewood Cliffs, N.J.: Prentice-Hall, Inc., 1969.

Haga, Enoch, *Understanding Automation*. Wheaton, Ill.: The Business Press, 1966.

Harvill, John B., *Basic Fortran Programing*. Englewood Cliffs, N.J.: Prentice-Hall, Inc., 1968.

Healy, Jeremiah J. and Dalward J. DeBruzzi, *Basic Fortran IV Programing*. Reading, Mass.: Addison-Wesley Publ. Co., 1968.

Honeywell, *Introduction to Electronic Data Processing*, a programed text. Wellesley Hills, Mass.: Honeywell, 1969.

Inman, Kenneth L., *Fundamentals of Electronic Data Processing*, a programed text. Englewood Cliffs, N.J.: Prentice-Hall, 1965.

Laskow, Robert and A. N. Feldzamen, *Bright Future Careers With Computers*. Phila., Pa.: Chilton Book Co., 1969.

Levine, Stanley L., *Computer Numbering Systems and Binary Arithmetic*, a programed text. New York, N.Y.: John F. Rider, 1965.

Lott, Richard W., *Basic Data Processing*. Englewood Cliffs, N.J.: Prentice-Hall, 1967.

Lytel, Allan, *ABC's of Boolean Algebra*. Indianapolis, Ind.: Howard W. Sams and Co., 1966.

Lytel, Allan, *ABC's of Computer Programing*. Indianapolis, Ind.: Howard W. Sams and Co., 1964.

Lytel, Allan, *Fundamentals of Data Processing*. Indianapolis, Ind.: Howard W. Sams and Co., 1964.

Marks, Robert W., *Simplifying Computer Mathematics*, a programed text. New York, N.Y.: Bantam (Unifact), 1968.

Murphy, John S., *Basics of Digital Computers*. New York, N.Y.: John F. Rider, 1967. Requires some previous knowledge of basic electronics.

Nashelsky, Louis, *Digital Computer Theory*. New York, N.Y.: John Wiley and Sons, Inc., 1966.

O'Neal, Leeland R., *Electronic Data Processing Systems*, a self instructional programed manual. Englewood Cliffs, N.J.: Prentice-Hall, 1964.

Organick, Elliott I., *A Fortran IV Primer*. Reading, Mass.: Addison-Wesley Publ. Co., 1966.

RCA Information Systems, *Introduction to Electronic Data Processing*, a self study training manual. Cherry Hill, N.J.: RCA Corp., 1967.

Saxon, James A. and Wesley W. Steyer, *Basic Principles of Data Processing,* second ed. Englewood Cliffs, N.J.: Prentice-Hall, 1970.

Science Research Associates, *Computer Concepts;* text, instructor's guide, classroom problems and exercises. Chicago, Ill.: Science Research Associates, an IBM subsidiary, 1970.

Science Research Associates, *Principles of Business Data Processing;* text, instructor's guide, classroom problems and exercises. Chicago, Ill.: Science Research Associates, an IBM subsidiary, 1970.

Seligsohn, I. J., *Your Career in Computer Programing.* New York, N.Y.: Julian Messner, 1967.

Sharpe, William F., *An Introduction to Computer Programing Using the Basic Language.* New York, N.Y.: Macmillan Co., 1967.

Smith, Robert E., *Discovering BASIC: A Problem Solving Approach.* New York, N.Y.: Hayden Book Co., 1970.

Spitzbarth, Laurel M., *Basic Cobol Programing,* self instruction manual and text. Reading, Mass.: Addison-Wesley Publ. Co., 1970.

Technical Education and Management, Inc., *Computer Basics,* a six-volume series requiring some previous knowledge of basic electronics. Indianapolis, Ind.: Howard W. Sams, 1962.

Truitt, Thomas D. and A. E. Rogers, *Basics of Analog Computers,* requires some previous knowledge of basic electronics. New York, N.Y.: John F. Rider, 1960.

U.S. Department of Labor, Bureau of Employment Security, *Occupations in Electronic Computing Systems* Washington, D.C. 20402: U.S. Government Printing Office, 1965, 40¢.

Weiss, Eric A., editor, *Computer Usage/Fundamentals.* New York, N.Y.: McGraw-Hill Book Co., 1969.

Wendell, Thomas M. and William H. Williams, *Introduction to Data Processing and Cobol,* beginning college level. New York, N.Y.: McGraw-Hill Book Co., 1969.

INDEX

159